# 19th Annual Meeting of the Young Researchers' Roundtable on Spoken Dialogue Systems (YRRSDS 2023)



Prague, Czech Republic
11-12 September 2023

ISBN: 978-1-7138-9066-9

**Printed from e-media with permission by:**

Curran Associates, Inc.
57 Morehouse Lane
Red Hook, NY 12571

**Some format issues inherent in the e-media version may also appear in this print version.**



Printed with permission by Curran Associates, Inc. (2025)



Association for Computational Linguistics
209 N. Eighth Street
Stroudsburg, Pennsylvania 18360

Phone: 1-570-476-8006
Fax: 1-570-476-0860

acl@aclweb.org

**Additional copies of this publication are available from:**

Curran Associates, Inc.
57 Morehouse Lane
Red Hook, NY 12571 USA
Phone: 845-758-0400
Fax: 845-758-2633
Email: curran@proceedings.com
Web: www.proceedings.com

YRRSDS 2023

# The 19th Annual Meeting of the Young Researchers' Roundtable on Spoken Dialogue Systems

## Proceedings of the Workshop

September 11 - 12, 2023
Prague, Czechia

Association for Computational Linguistics (ACL)
209 N. Eighth Street
Stroudsburg, PA 18360
USA
Tel: +1-570-476-8006
Fax: +1-570-476-0860
acl@aclweb.org

**Sponsor**

Omilia
Conversational Intelligence

**In Collaboration With**

CHARLES UNIVERSITY

SIGdial

# Preface

We are delighted to provide the opening words for the proceedings of the 19th Young Researchers Roundtable on Spoken Dialogue Systems (YRRSDS) 2023, a workshop on Spoken Dialogue Systems for PhDs, PostDocs and New Researchers. YRRSDS 2023 was collocated with the Special Interest Group on Discourse and Dialogue (SIGDIAL) 2023. The workshop took place on September 11-12, 2023 in Prague, Czech Republic at the OREA Hotel Pyramida. This year, the format for YRRSDS was in person.

Submissions to YRRSDS consisted of writing a 2 page position paper outlining the young researcher's current research topic and interests, and general points they would like to see discussed during the roundtable sessions in the workshop.

Each submission was reviewed by 2 senior researchers from our Advisory Committee. We are immensely grateful to the members of the Advisory Committee for their excellent and thoughtful reviews. Their contributions have been essential to providing critical feedback to the participants of the workshop during this stage in their career.

Participants accepted to the program were required to present a poster based on their submission. This year, YRRSDS accepted all 25 submissions that were received.

The roundtable discussions this year focused on the following topics: Large Language Models (LLMs), Evaluation methods in Spoken Dialogue Systems, Knowledge Bases, Reasoning & Planning, Multi-modality & Interaction, Architectures and Ethics, Privacy & Regulations.

In addition to the poster sessions and roundtables, the program consisted of 3 fantastic keynote presentations. We would like to take this opportunity to thank and acknowledge our 3 keynote speakers: Verena Rieser (Senior Staff Research Scientist at Google DeepMind, hon. Professor at Heriot-Watt University and Co-Founder at ALANA AI), Malihe Alikhani (Assistant Professor of AI and social justice at the Khoury School of Computer Science, Northeastern University) and David Traum (Director for Natural Language Research at the Institute for Creative Technologies and Research Professor at USC Viterbi School of Engineering Computer Science Department) for their inspiring talks.

We thank the organisers who ensured that the conference ran very smoothly, and was enjoyed by all participants. We gratefully acknowledge the support of our sponsor: Omilia Conversational Intelligence.

Lastly, we are excited to announce that this year will mark the first year the YRRSDS proceedings will be integrated as part of the ACL anthology. We hope that by integrating the proceedings in this way, young researchers will have the opportunity to have visibility on their positional submission, and by extension their research.

*Tanvi Dinkar and Javier Chiyah-Garcia, Organizing Committee YRRSDS 2023*

# Organizing Committee

**Organizers:**

**Vojtěch Hudeček**

Charles University

**Patrícia Schmidtová**

Charles University

**Tanvi Dinkar**

Heriot-Watt University

**Weronika Sieińska**

Heriot-Watt University

**Javier Chiyah-Garcia**

Heriot-Watt University

**Advisory committee:**

Srinivas Bangalore, *Interactions LLC*

Timo Baumann, *University of Hamburg, OTH Regensburg*

Luciana Benotti, *National University of Córdoba*

Hendrik Buschmeier, *Bielefeld University*

Justine Cassell, *PRAIRIE Paris Artificial Intelligence Research Institute in INRIA Paris*

Nina Dethlefs, *University of Hull*

Luis Fernando D'Haro Enríquez, *Technical University of Madrid*

Kallirroi Georgila, *University of Southern California*

Larry Heck, *Viv Labs*

Ryuichiro Higashinaka, *Nagoya University*

Julia Hirschberg, *Columbia University*

Krzysztof Jassem, *Adam Mickiewicz University*

Tatsuya Kawahara, *Kyoto University*

James Kennedy, *Disney Research*

Kazunori Komatani, *Osaka University*

Ioannis Konstas, *Heriot-Watt University*

Udo Kruschwitz, *Regensburg University*

Marek Kubis, *Adam Mickiewicz University*

Jackson Liscombe, *Modality AI*

Pierre Lison, *Norwegian Computing Centre*

Wolfgang Minker, *University of Ulm*

Sebastian Möller, *Technical University of Berlin*

Mikio Nakano, *C4A Research Institute*

Diarmuid Ó Séaghdha, *Apple*

Alexandros Papangelis, *Amazon Alexa AI*

Vikram Ramanarayanan, *Modality AI*

Abhinav Rastogi, *Google*

Giuseppe Riccardi, *University of Trento*

David Schlangen, *University of Potsdam*

Gabriel Skantze, *KTH Royal Institute of Technology*

Paweł Skórzewski, *Adam Mickiewicz University*

David Traum, *University of Southern California*

Khiet Truong, *University of Twente*

Stefan Ultes, *University of Bamberg*

Marilyn Walker, *University of California, Santa Cruz*

Nigel Ward, *University of Texas at El Paso*

Michael White, *Ohio State University*

Zhou Yu, *Columbia University*

# Organizers' Notes of the Roundtable Discussions

## Ethics, Privacy & Regulations

The meeting's primary focus revolved around the ethical aspects of privacy, regulation, and human interaction with virtual systems. The conversation began with a deep dive into privacy, highlighting the delicate balance between privacy and utility. Participants stressed the importance of making informed choices when it comes to cookies and being aware of how data is used, especially with virtual systems that can blur the lines. An interesting point was raised about data usage by companies, as some have recently updated their policies regarding collecting user data based on input queries into LLMs.

Anthropomorphism in dialogue systems emerged as another important topic. The use of human-like language to describe these systems, along with customizable chatbots, raised questions about how users perceive these systems and the impact on the community. The need for clarifying the relationship between users and the system was emphasised, with user studies to explore confirmation bias when integrating users into the dialogue process.

## Architecture

The meeting involved a discussion on end-to-end (E2E) systems versus modular systems in dialogue systems, with E2E systems increasingly becoming the standard while modular systems are less favoured. However, E2E systems have issues related to low interpretability. The question of whether Language Models (LLMs) are better suited than modular architectures for production environments was raised, with the consensus that LLMs tend to work efficiently, even with small amounts of data. The discussion also touched on the trade-off between the size and speed of integrating LLMs in a dialogue system. In the context of transformers, memory constraints and limitations were examined, highlighting their short memory, which can be a limitation in dialogue settings unless trained with large sequence lengths.

## Large Language Models

During the meeting, the attendees discussed the suitability of Language Models (LLMs) specifically applied to Spoken Dialogue Systems (SDS). Some researchers discussed their experiences with multi-party dialogues, where LLMs surprisingly demonstrated effectiveness in various conversational scenarios. This raised questions about the potential practical applications of LLMs in complex dialogue systems.

However, the real-world deployment of LLMs raised concerns. One significant issue was hallucinations, where LLMs generate information that is incorrect or entirely fictional. These hallucinations can be problematic and affect the reliability of the model's output. Also discussed were the consequences of training LLMs with synthetic data generated by other LLMs, emphasising potential complications and unintended outcomes. The discussion shifted to the uncertainty surrounding the data used to train LLMs, as well as the risk of data contamination. It remains unclear what information these models have been exposed to during training. Another concerning aspect was the overconfidence of LLMs in their answers. This underscores the importance of fact-checking and ensuring the reliability of information provided by these models.

Despite these challenges, the meeting recognized the positive impacts of LLMs. They can be valuable in tasks like enhancing the fluency and functionality of dialogue systems. High-quality English LLMs can assist in language learning and provide access to knowledge. Furthermore, LLMs have demonstrated strengths in picking up on nuances in task-oriented dialogues.

Finally, the conversation touched on fundamental limitations in LLM architecture. Predicting the next word was considered a limitation, especially when dealing with long-context dialogues and multi-modal tasks.These limitations were central to the debate surrounding the overall capabilities and potential constraints of LLMs in the field of dialogue and communication.

## Evaluation

The discussion started with a focus on the quality of evaluations conducted by crowd workers and the inherent challenges when utilising Mechanical Turk for human evaluations in Natural Language Processing (NLP). Anecdotes about experiences with Mechanical Turk were shared, shedding light on issues related to privacy and high rejection rates. The challenges of managing rejection rates and compensation for incomplete tasks on Mechanical Turk were explored in detail.

As the dialogue progressed, various crowd-sourcing platforms, including alternatives like Prolific, were brought into consideration for specific survey needs and participant selection. This shift highlighted the need for identifying and filtering out low-quality annotators, with attention checks and quality control measures being proposed as potential solutions. The conversation also delved into the reproducibility of human evaluations, even for apparently objective tasks such as fluency and grammaticality.

Lastly, the granularity of annotations for dialogue research was discussed; i.e. shifting from collecting annotations at the system-level to the turn-level. The conversation also discussed the idea of collecting diverse opinions from annotators and employing distributional approaches to assess model performance.

## Knowledge Bases, Reasoning & Planning

The discussion centred around how to create solutions to dynamically update or access knowledge within LLMs that have been integrated into spoken dialogue systems. Since information is constantly evolving, having a static knowledge base can lead to outdated and inaccurate responses in a dialogue system.

We also discussed whether querying LLMs with specific knowledge requests or adopting more complex integration methods would be more effective for dialogue systems. The choice between these approaches is pivotal as it impacts the user experience and the reliability of information provided.

However, a significant concern that emerged during our discussion was that LLMs produce hallucinations and generate responses that are factually incorrect or misleading.

## Multi-Modality & Interaction

The discussion was centred around the nature of multi-modal conversations, which is very subjective. The limitations of using only text was emphasised, especially in capturing the contextual cues of dialogue, such as speech, tone, and prosody, highlighting how multimodal cues have the potential to alter conversation meanings.

It was noted that many works claim multi-modality, even when they predominantly involve image and text, indicating that the term has become somewhat overused.

A question posed was whether multi-modality could provide the missing context in current spoken dialogue systems. Examples of multi-modality in spoken dialogue systems were then shared. It was stressed that integrating multi-modality into SDS is crucial, but significantly more challenging compared to non-interactive models.

# Table of Contents

# Conference Program

**Monday, September 11, 2023**

**09:30–09:45 Registration and Poster Setup**

**09:45–10:00 Welcome**

**10:00–10:30 Industry Keynote: Omilia (Gold Sponsor) by Vojtěch Hudeček**

**10:30–11:00 Coffee Break**

**11:00–12:00 Poster Session 1**

*Processing Referential Ambiguities in Situated Dialogue Systems*
Javier Chiyah-Garcia

*Safety and Robustness in Conversational AI*
Tanvi Dinkar

*Incremental Speech Processing for Voice Assistant Accessibility*
Angus Addlesee

*Advancing Spoken Dialog Systems for Manufacturing: From Conceptual Architecture and Taxonomy to Real Case Applications and Future Directions*
Silvia Colabianchi

*Conversational Grounding in Multimodal Dialog Systems*
Biswesh Mohapatra

*SQL Comment Generation and Additional Research Interests*
Alyssa Allen

*On Referring Language Use in Visually Grounded Dialogue*
Bram Willemsen

**Monday, September 11, 2023 (continued)**

*Challenges and Approaches in Designing Social SDS in the LLM Era*
Koji Inoue

*Breakdowns and Repairs. Detecting Patterns that Lead to Breakdowns in Customer Service Messages*
Anouck Braggaar

*Towards More Natural Dialogues: Integrating Open-Domain Dialogue Skills into Task-Oriented Agents*
Armand Stricker

*The Future of Designing Spoken Dialogue Systems and Analyzing Written Conversations*
Livia Qian

*Exploring the Synergy of Deep Learning and Anthropomorphism in Multimodal Dialogue Systems*
Iwona Christop

**12:00–12:30** **Roundtable Session 1: Ethics, Privacy & Regulations**
Chairs: Tanvi Dinkar, Patrícia Schmidtová

**12:00–12:30** **Roundtable Session 1: Architecture**
Chair: Javier Chiyah-Garcia

**12:30–13:30** **Lunch**

**13:30–14:30** **Poster Session 2**

*A Perspective on Anchoring and Dialogue History Propagation for Smoother Interactions with Spoken Task-Oriented Dialogue Systems*
Lucas Druart

*More Human-Like Interaction in Spoken Dialogue Systems: Global Context for Natural Language Understanding and Multimodal Solutions*
Kacper Dudzic

*Designing and Evaluating LLM-based Conversational Agents for Behaviour Change*
Selina Meyer

**Monday, September 11, 2023 (continued)**

| | |
|---|---|
| **14:30–15:15** | **Keynote: A short history of data-driven dialogue systems in 5 acts: Where do we go from here? by Verena Rieser** |
| **15:15–15:45** | **Coffee Break** |
| **15:45–16:30** | **Roundtable Session 2: Large Language Models** |
| **19:30** | **Dinner** |

**Tuesday, September 12, 2023**

| | |
|---|---|
| **09:30–09:45** | **Welcome** |
| **09:45–10:30** | **Roundtable Session 3: Evaluation**<br>Chairs: Patrícia Schmidtová, Tanvi Dinkar |
| **09:45–10:30** | **Roundtable Session 3: Emotion, Empathy & Personalised Dialogues**<br>Chair: Vojtěch Hudeček |
| **10:30–11:00** | **Coffee Break** |
| **11:00–11:45** | **Roundtable Session 4: Knowledge Bases, Reasoning & Planning**<br>Chair: Vojtěch Hudeček |

**Tuesday, September 12, 2023 (continued)**

| | |
|---|---|
| **11:00–11:45** | **Roundtable Session 4: Multi-Modality & Interaction**<br>Chair: Javier Chiyah-Garcia |
| **11:45–12:30** | **Keynote: The past, present, and future of dialogue systems and advice to young researchers by David Traum** |
| **12:30–13:30** | **Lunch** |
| **13:30–14:00** | **Group Photo** |
| **14:00–14:45** | **Keynote: Leveraging Generative AI for Inclusive and Equitable Dialogue Systems by Malihe Alikhani** |
| **14:45–15:00** | **Closing** |
| **15:00** | **Free Discussion** |

# Keynotes

## Keynote 1: A short history of data-driven dialogue systems in 5 acts: Where do we go from here?

*Verena Rieser*

*Senior Staff Research Scientist at Google DeepMind, hon. Professor at Heriot-Watt University and Co-Founder at ALANA AI*

**Bio:** Verena is a Senior Staff Research Scientist at Google DeepMind, where she works on Safer Conversational AI. She is also honorary professor at Heriot-Watt University in Edinburgh and a co-founder of the Conversational AI company ALANA AI. Verena holds a PhD from Saarland University in Germany and a MSc from the University of Edinburgh, where she also spent time as a postdoctoral researcher.

She has 20 years of experience in developing and researching data-driven conversational systems. In the early 2000s she developed a series of breakthrough innovations that laid the groundwork for statistical dialogue control using Reinforcement Learning. More recently, Verena and her team pioneered work on identifying and addressing safety risks in neural conversational systems, which was awarded with a Leverhulme Senior Research Fellowship by the Royal Society.

**Keynote 2: The past, present, and future of dialogue systems and advice to young researchers**

*David Traum*

*Director for Natural Language Research at the Institute for Creative Technologies (ICT) and Research Professor at USC Viterbi School of Engineering Computer Science Department*

**Bio:** David Traum is a principal scientist at ICT and a research faculty member at the Department of Computer Science at USC. At ICT, Traum leads the Natural Language Dialogue Group, which consists of seven Ph.D.s, four students, and four other researchers.

The group engages in research in all aspects of natural language dialogue, including dialogue management, spoken and natural language understanding and generation and dialogue evaluation. In addition, the group collaborates with others at ICT and elsewhere on integrated virtual humans, and transitioning natural language dialogue capability for use in training and other interactive applications.

Traum's research focuses on dialogue communication between human and artificial agents. He has engaged in theoretical, implementational and empirical approaches to the problem, studying human-human natural language and multi-modal dialogue, as well as building a number of dialogue systems to communicate with human users.

He has pioneered several research thrusts in computational dialogue modeling, including computational models of grounding (how common ground is established through conversation), the information state approach to dialogue, multiparty dialogue, and non-cooperative dialogue.

Traum is author of over 200 technical articles, is a founding editor of the Journal Dialogue and Discourse, has chaired and served on many conference program committees, and is currently the president emeritus of SIGDIAL, the international special interest group in discourse and dialogue. He earned his Ph.D. in computer science at University of Rochester in 1994.

## Keynote 3: Leveraging Generative AI for Inclusive and Equitable Dialogue Systems

*Malihe Alikhani*

*Assistant Professor of AI and social justice at the Khoury School of Computer Science, Northeastern University*

**Bio:** Malihe Alikhani is an Assistant Professor at the Khoury School of Computer Science, Northeastern University. She earned her Ph.D. in computer science with a graduate certificate in cognitive science from Rutgers University in 2020. Her research interests center on using representations of communicative structure, machine learning, and cognitive science to design equitable and inclusive language technologies. This involves developing systems that can communicate and collaborate with diverse populations, especially those from underserved communities, for critical applications such as education, health, and social justice. Her work has received best paper awards at ACL 2021, UAI2022, INLG2021, and UMAP2022 and has been supported by DARPA, NIH, Google, and Amazon.

**Javier Chiyah-Garcia**

Heriot-Watt University
Edinburgh, Scotland
United Kingdom

fjc3@hw.ac.uk
https://jchiyah.github.io

## 1 Research interests

Conversations between humans are based on the collection of mutual knowledge, experiences, beliefs, assumptions and even goals of the interlocutors. We estimate these unconsciously, but they attribute meaning outside words that is crucial to understanding the interaction. This common grounding is what connects the meaning of the physical world with our language abstractions (Harnad, 1990). However, current intelligent systems do not share this mutual understanding and common grounding, heavily impairing the interaction. Users have to simplify queries, be more explicit and repeat information already mentioned so that their language matches the way that dialogue systems communicate.

As previous works have demonstrated, dialogue models trained on large scale datasets are not able to capture meaning beyond words (symbols) (Bisk et al., 2020; Bender and Koller, 2020; Bender et al., 2021) and thus fall short on tasks that require common sense or understanding nuanced meanings. Training on text alone or even text and images may not be enough to continue advancing in the field further. Spoken dialogue systems (SDSs) operate with a different view of the world from us and thus, struggle to draw connections between what can be observed or the result of actions and language, resulting in poor interactions.

### 1.1 Situated human-robot interaction

My research interests lie in the area of **situated interaction** in environments where robots and humans are co-located as part of my PhD. In these settings, **natural language instructions** given by a human can be rooted in surrounding objects, the dialogue history and even previous events. Therefore, human-robot interactions in situated environments requires agents to maintain appropriate situation awareness, which a dialogue system trained on text alone may not be suited to (Bisk et al., 2020).

As other fields related to interaction, such as computer vision or gesture recognition, start to reach maturity with efficient and high-performing off-the-shelf tools, it is important to incorporate these with SDS. A more holistic approach that combines dialogue, world state and other interaction modalities may yield better interactive systems and solve some shortfalls of the current field, such as the large amounts of training data needed or the disconnection between virtual and physical world. Previous works have proposed training models that combine natural language with visuals and world state to spur grounding (Bisk et al., 2016; Mei et al., 2016; Tan and Bansal, 2018; Suhr et al., 2019a; Shridhar et al., 2020; Padmakumar et al., 2021), yet most of them focus on understanding well-formed instructions sequentially, as opposed to fluid, unpredictable or noisy dialogues as with real-world conditions. In these cases and unlike current SDS, humans are able to collaborate and adapt, asking for clarifications or help when needed.

### 1.2 Referential ambiguities

Of particular relevance to situated dialogues are **referential ambiguities**, which arise when a referring expression does not uniquely identify the intended referent for the addressee. They signal a potential mismatch between the perspectives of the speaker and hearer (see e.g., Dobnik et al. (2015)) and thus hamper the interaction (e.g., not finding the correct object or resolving an action). Upon detecting such ambiguities, we engage in subsequent meta-communicative clarificational exchanges (Purver, 2004) to repair the miscommunication (Purver et al., 2018).

My current work explores the use of state-of-the-art models to **resolve referential ambiguities** in multi-modal dialogues. We use the SIMMC 2.0 dataset (Kottur et al., 2021), where a conversational agent helps a user pick items to shop in a virtual shared environment. The agent needs to answer queries and perform instructions as well as keep track of the items mentioned throughout the dialogue in a multi-modal scene. Due to the high amount of similar-looking objects and long dialogues with dynamic objectives, the user needs to employ rich referring expressions, which commonly cause ambiguities in both the visual and conversational contexts (see Figure 1).

Initial analyses into the clarificational exchanges that arise suggest that models struggle to understand and resolve these ambiguities compared to other coreferences. This follows my work from the past year in vision and language models for detecting these ambiguities and resolving coreferences in multi-modal dialogues that led to Chiyah-Garcia et al. (2022). Vision and language models



*Proceedings of the 19th Annual Meeting of the Young Reseachers' Roundtable on Spoken Dialogue Systems*, pages 1–4
September 11–12, 2023. ©2023 Association for Computational Linguistics

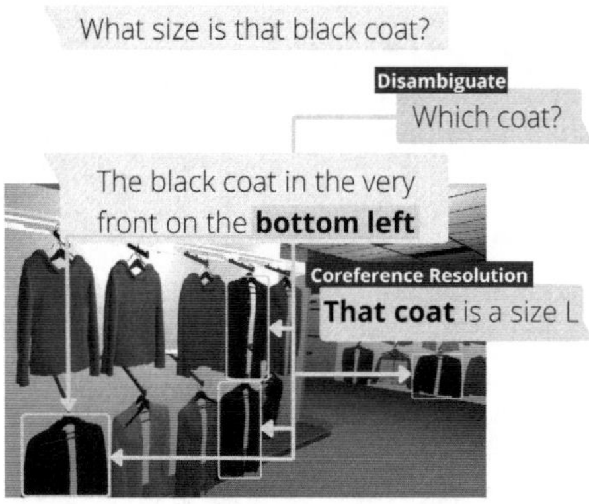


Figure 1: Example dialogue from the SIMMC 2.0 dataset where the system engages in a clarificational exchange to find the correct coat mentioned by the user.

are not enough, as they do not easily carry information across turns and/or are able to ground the information to the objects in the scene.

Future work will focus on learning the signals required to process clarifications and suitable architectures in the context of situated multi-modal interactions. Vision and language models, although promising, lack the relational information needed to fully ground both modalities in complex environments. Models that learn disentangled object representations (Bengio et al., 2013) could be better at exploiting the attributes of potential referential candidates and ultimately be better suited at resolving ambiguities in increasingly unstructured and multi-modal scenarios.

### 1.3 Past work

My current work on situated human-robot interaction with SDS builds upon my previous work in explainable dialogue systems to operate remote autonomous vehicles (Chiyah Garcia et al., 2018a,b, 2020a), automatically generating natural language explanations of learned robot behaviour (Chiyah Garcia et al., 2021) and analysing the use of crowd-sourced versus lab-collected data (Chiyah Garcia et al., 2020b; Lopes et al., 2020) for bootstrapping human-robot dialogue systems in the domain of emergency response.

## 2 SDS research

The field of dialogue research should work more closely with other fields related to interaction. Dialogue systems trained on text alone cannot fully understand the nuances of language and how these affect the physical world, hence works are increasingly combining natural language and rich image representations to improve text and vision benchmarks (Das et al., 2018; Suhr et al., 2019b; Zellers et al., 2019; Shridhar et al., 2020; Padmakumar et al., 2021). Improved multi-modal representations or more complete world views may be crucial for SDS to navigate more complex scenarios.

SDS could also become more robust and flexible in the way that they process natural language. Incrementally processing words instead of turns could enable SDSs to better understand and coordinate the conversation with a human (Schlangen and Skantze, 2009; Eshghi et al., 2015), as we often use feedback mechanisms such as backchannels (i.e., 'okay' or 'mhm') or clarifications to signal what has been grounded in a dialogue. Fluid human-robot interactions may require keeping track of the conversation context explicitly in real-time (Hough and Schlangen, 2016) so the SDS can self-repair the state when there are issues or misunderstandings (Hough, 2015).

Finally, the field of SDS could explore new ways of blending the natural language element of interactions with other modalities beyond vision, such as non-verbal communication. Agents that only understand words may not be suitable to interactions outside labs and in unstructured environments.

## 3 Suggested topics for discussion

Here are some of the topics for discussion:

- **Multi-modality** in SDS design, how to represent other modalities aside from language and how to use this to track the dialogue context.
- The rise of **large language models** such as GPT-4 and the challenges and opportunities that they bring to SDS.
- **Situated human-agent interaction**, where the agent can both observe and modify the world. Human-robot collaboration through natural language is a related sub-topic.
- **Incremental natural language understanding** either through a mix of semantic and statistical or pure methods.

## References

Emily M. Bender, Timnit Gebru, Angelina McMillan-Major, and Shmargaret Shmitchell. 2021. On the dangers of stochastic parrots: Can language models be too big? In *Proceedings of the 2021 ACM Conference on Fairness, Accountability, and Transparency*. Association for Computing Machinery, New York, NY, USA, FAccT '21, page 610–623. https://doi.org/10.1145/3442188.3445922.

Emily M. Bender and Alexander Koller. 2020. Climbing towards NLU: On meaning, form, and understanding in the age of data. In *Proceedings of the 58th Annual Meeting of the Association for Computational Linguistics*. Association for Computational Linguistics, Online, pages 5185–5198. https://doi.org/10.18653/v1/2020.acl-main.463.

Yoshua Bengio, Aaron Courville, and Pascal Vincent. 2013. Representation learning: A review and new perspectives. *IEEE transactions on pattern analysis and machine intelligence* 35(8):1798–1828.

Yonatan Bisk, Ari Holtzman, Jesse Thomason, Jacob Andreas, Yoshua Bengio, Joyce Chai, Mirella Lapata, Angeliki Lazaridou, Jonathan May, Aleksandr Nisnevich, Nicolas Pinto, and Joseph Turian. 2020. Experience grounds language. In *Proceedings of the 2020 Conference on Empirical Methods in Natural Language Processing (EMNLP)*. Association for Computational Linguistics, Online, pages 8718–8735. https://doi.org/10.18653/v1/2020.emnlp-main.703.

Yonatan Bisk, Deniz Yuret, and Daniel Marcu. 2016. Natural language communication with robots. In *Proceedings of the 2016 Conference of the North American Chapter of the Association for Computational Linguistics: Human Language Technologies*. Association for Computational Linguistics, San Diego, California, pages 751–761. https://doi.org/10.18653/v1/N16-1089.

Francisco Javier Chiyah Garcia, José Lopes, and Helen Hastie. 2020a. Natural language interaction to facilitate mental models of remote robots. In *Proceedings of the Workshop on Mental Models of Robots, HRI'20*. ACM, Cambridge, UK, HRI'20.

Francisco Javier Chiyah Garcia, José Lopes, Xingkun Liu, and Helen Hastie. 2020b. CRWIZ: A framework for crowdsourcing real-time Wizard-of-Oz dialogues. In *Proceedings of the 12th Language Resources and Evaluation Conference*. European Language Resources Association, Marseille, France, pages 288–297. https://www.aclweb.org/anthology/2020.lrec-1.36.

Francisco Javier Chiyah Garcia, David A. Robb, Atanas Laskov, Xingkun Liu, Pedro Patron, and Helen Hastie. 2018a. Explainable autonomy: A study of explanation styles for building clear mental models. In *Proceedings of The 11th International Natural Language Generation Conference*. ACM, Tilburg, The Netherlands, INLG'18, pages 99–108. http://www.aclweb.org/anthology/W18-65.

Francisco Javier Chiyah Garcia, David A. Robb, X. Liu, Atanas Laskov, Patron Patron, and Helen Hastie. 2018b. Explain yourself: A natural language interface for scrutable autonomous robots. In *Proceedings of Explainable Robotic Systems Workshop*. Chicago, IL, USA, HRI'18.

Francisco Javier Chiyah Garcia, Simón C. Smith, José Lopes, Subramanian Ramamoorthy, and Helen Hastie. 2021. Self-explainable robots in remote environments. In *Companion of the 2021 ACM/IEEE International Conference on Human-Robot Interaction*. Association for Computing Machinery, New York, NY, USA, HRI '21 Companion, page 662–664. https://doi.org/10.1145/3434074.3447275.

Javier Chiyah-Garcia, Alessandro Suglia, José David Lopes, Arash Eshghi, and Helen Hastie. 2022. Exploring multi-modal representations for ambiguity detection & coreference resolution in the simmc 2.0 challenge. In *AAAI 2022 DSTC10 Workshop*.

Abhishek Das, Samyak Datta, Georgia Gkioxari, Stefan Lee, Devi Parikh, and Dhruv Batra. 2018. Embodied Question Answering. In *Proceedings of the IEEE Conference on Computer Vision and Pattern Recognition (CVPR)*.

Simon Dobnik, Christine Howes, and John Kelleher. 2015. Changing perspective: Local alignment of reference frames in dialogue. In *Proceedings of the 19th Workshop on the Semantics and Pragmatics of Dialogue - Full Papers*. SEMDIAL, Gothenburg, Sweden. http://semdial.org/anthology/Z15-Dobnik_semdial_0006.pdf.

Arash Eshghi, Christine Howes, Eleni Gregoromichelaki, Julian Hough, and Matthew Purver. 2015. Feedback in conversation as incremental semantic update. In *IWCS 2015 - Proceedings of the 11th International Conference on Computational Semantics*. Association for Computational Linguistics, pages 261–271.

Stevan Harnad. 1990. The symbol grounding problem. *Physica D: Nonlinear Phenomena* 42(1-3):335–346. https://doi.org/10.1016/0167-2789(90)90087-6.

Julian Hough. 2015. *Modelling Incremental Self-Repair Processing in Dialogue*. Ph.D. thesis, Queen Mary University of London.

Julian Hough and David Schlangen. 2016. Investigating Fluidity for Human-Robot Interaction with Real-time, Real-world Grounding Strategies. In *Proceedings of the 17th Annual Meeting of the Special Interest Group on Discourse and Dialogue*. Association for Computational Linguistics, Stroudsburg, PA, USA, September, pages 288–298. https://doi.org/10.18653/v1/W16-3637.

Satwik Kottur, Seungwhan Moon, Alborz Geramifard, and Babak Damavandi. 2021. SIMMC 2.0: A task-oriented dialog dataset for immersive multimodal conversations. In *Proceedings of the 2021 Conference on*

*Empirical Methods in Natural Language Processing*. Association for Computational Linguistics, Online and Punta Cana, Dominican Republic, pages 4903–4912. https://aclanthology.org/2021.emnlp-main.401.

José Lopes, Francisco Javier Chiyah Garcia, and Helen Hastie. 2020. The lab vs the crowd: An investigation into data quality for neural dialogue models. In *Workshop on Human in the Loop Dialogue Systems at NeurIPS 2020*. https://arxiv.org/abs/2012.03855.

Hongyuan Mei, Mohit Bansal, and R. Matthew Walter. 2016. Listen, attend, and walk: Neural mapping of navigational instructions to action sequences. In *30th AAAI Conference on Artificial Intelligence, AAAI 2016*. AAAI press, pages 2772–2778. http://arxiv.org/abs/1506.04089.

Aishwarya Padmakumar, Jesse Thomason, Ayush Shrivastava, Patrick Lange, Anjali Narayan-Chen, Spandana Gella, Robinson Piramithu, Gokhan Tur, and Dilek Hakkani-Tur. 2021. TEACh: Task-driven Embodied Agents that Chat. In *arXiv:2110.00534 [Cs]*.

Matthew Purver. 2004. *The Theory and Use of Clarification Requests in Dialogue*. Ph.D. thesis, University of London.

Matthew Purver, Julian Hough, and Christing Howes. 2018. Computational models of miscommunication phenomena. *Cognitive Science* 10(2):425–451. https://doi.org/10.1111/tops.12324.

David Schlangen and Gabriel Skantze. 2009. A general, abstract model of incremental dialogue processing. In *Proceedings of the 12th Conference of the European Chapter of the ACL (EACL 2009)*. Association for Computational Linguistics, Athens, Greece, pages 710–718. https://www.aclweb.org/anthology/E09-1081.

Mohit Shridhar, Jesse Thomason, Daniel Gordon, Yonatan Bisk, Winson Han, Roozbeh Mottaghi, Luke Zettlemoyer, and Dieter Fox. 2020. ALFRED: A Benchmark for Interpreting Grounded Instructions for Everyday Tasks. In *The IEEE Conference on Computer Vision and Pattern Recognition (CVPR)*. https://arxiv.org/abs/1912.01734.

Alane Suhr, Claudia Yan, Jack Schluger, Stanley Yu, Hadi Khader, Marwa Mouallem, Iris Zhang, and Yoav Artzi. 2019a. Executing Instructions in Situated Collaborative Interactions. In *Proceedings of the 2019 Conference on Empirical Methods in Natural Language Processing and the 9th International Joint Conference on Natural Language Processing (EMNLP-IJCNLP)*. Association for Computational Linguistics, Stroudsburg, PA, USA, pages 2119–2130. https://doi.org/10.18653/v1/D19-1218.

Alane Suhr, Stephanie Zhou, Ally Zhang, Iris Zhang, Huajun Bai, and Yoav Artzi. 2019b. A corpus for reasoning about natural language grounded in photographs. In *Proceedings of the 57th Annual Meeting of the Association for Computational Linguistics*. Association for Computational Linguistics, Florence, Italy, pages 6418–6428. https://doi.org/10.18653/v1/P19-1644.

Hao Tan and Mohit Bansal. 2018. Source-target inference models for spatial instruction understanding. In *32nd AAAI Conference on Artificial Intelligence, AAAI 2018*. AAAI press, pages 5504–5511. http://arxiv.org/abs/1707.03804.

Rowan Zellers, Yonatan Bisk, Ali Farhadi, and Yejin Choi. 2019. From recognition to cognition: Visual commonsense reasoning. In *2019 IEEE/CVF Conference on Computer Vision and Pattern Recognition (CVPR)*. pages 6713–6724. https://doi.org/10.1109/CVPR.2019.00688.

## Biographical sketch

Javier Chiyah-Garcia (he/him) is a PhD student at Heriot-Watt University working on human-robot collaboration using conversational agents. Currently, he is exploring methods of interaction with situated robots in smart factories with industry partner Siemens. Previously, he worked on the development of a dialogue system for remote operation of autonomous underwater vehicles, funded by the Ministry of Defence in the UK. He also explored how explanations affect the operator's mental model of the underwater vehicles. One of his goals is to make robots more intuitive to use through speech, and he is very excited about all the amazing things that human-robot teams can achieve together. After the PhD, he plans to join a research lab in industry to act as a bridge with academia and deploy more intuitive robots that make our lives a bit easier.

**Tanvi Dinkar**

Heriot-Watt University
Edinburgh,
Scotland,
EH14 4AS

t.dinkar@hw.ac.uk
animatas.eu/network/esr/tanvi/

## 1 Research interests

Recently there has been an explosion of chatbot-style systems that utilise Large Language Models (LLMs) deployed in the real world. However, with this large scale deployment, the safety of these systems is critical (Bommasani et al., 2021; Bender et al., 2021; Weidinger et al., 2021; Bergman et al., 2022; Dinan et al., 2022a). While the NLP community has traditionally explored the ethical issues of text-based models (such as hate speech detection, inherent biases of the system etc), real-world conversations and dialogues differ *significantly* from structured, written text documents, and this brings with it its own unique set of safety challenges.

Firstly, a central theme of generative linguistics going back to von Humboldt, is that language is 'an infinite use of finite means', i.e there exists many ways to say the same thing. However, current research fails to account for this inherent variability of language, which results in a **lack of robustness** of these systems to: real-world use cases, noisy perturbations to the input, or even adversarial attacks (Jin et al., 2019; Moradi and Samwald, 2021; Wu et al., 2021).

Additionally, in real-world interactions, words alone don't sufficiently communicate intended meaning; listeners often arrive at meaning inferring several other speaker cues, such as prosody or even context. However, these unique *human-like* ways to communicate may be coopted by designers of these systems to drive up user engagement, encouraging humans to relate to such systems in human-like ways – i.e. these systems are **anthropomorphised** or personified. Assigning human characteristics to dialogue systems can have consequences that could be on one hand, harmless, e.g. referring to automated systems by gender, but on the other, disastrous e.g., people following the advice or instructions of a system to do harm[1]. Based on these themes, I will present the research interests in my PostDoc (§1.1 and §1.2) on **safety and robustness** specific to **conversational AI**, including the relevant overlap from my PhD.

[1]A person recently has committed suicide, allegedly as a consequence of the harmful outputs generated from such a system (Xiang, 2023).

### 1.1 Robustness in Conversational AI: How do models perform in real-world conditions?

The real-world performance of text based models first interested me in my PhD, where I focused on how robust such models are to input transcripts arising from speech, given that they are pre-trained on massive amounts of written text. With this in mind, we investigated the representations of spontaneous speech phenomena present in speech transcripts – in particular fillers ('uh', 'um') – using deep contextualised word embeddings. A finding of the work was that Bi-directional Encoder Representations (BERT) (Devlin et al., 2019) already has existing representations of fillers, and their inclusion in the input decreased the uncertainty of the language model (Dinkar et al., 2020), despite research to suggest that other spontaneous speech phenomena increase uncertainty (Sen, 2020). Thus (somewhat surprisingly), LLMs may be robust to certain kinds of spontaneous speech phenomena.

In my post-doc I shifted focus to safety-critical contexts, deliberating on whether there are *scenarios where models **must be** robust to variability*. If so, what steps can be taken to ensure such guarantees? For the former question, it may be required legally for a chatbot to *always* disclose identity, such as California legislation stating *'[...] unlawful for a bot to mislead people about its artificial identity [...]'* (Legislature, 2018). Similar legislation could be widespread in the future (Montgomery, 2023). Another scenario is that a system may give a user false impressions of its 'expertise' and generate harmful advice in response to medically related user queries (Abercrombie and Rieser, 2022; Dinan et al., 2022b). In practice it may be desirable for the system recognise medical queries and avoid answering them. Thus the question remains, on how to create and ensure such guarantees for the output, given the inherent variability of language?

I collaborated with researchers to analyse the feasibility of applying formal verification methods to the NLP domain (work under review). These methods *ensure* that for every possible input, the output generated by a neural network satisfies the desired properties (such as consistently disclosing non-human identity). The work proposed semantically informed verification filters, which



*Proceedings of the 19th Annual Meeting of the Young Reseachers' Roundtable on Spoken Dialogue Systems*, pages 5–8
September 11–12, 2023. ©2023 Association for Computational Linguistics

essentially creates a geometric shape around a certain embedded input in a pre-trained LLM (such as a query 'are you a chatbot'), and *guarantees* that for every data point surrounding that input within that shape, the output of the network will generate the desired class (i.e. confirming non-human identity). We evaluated the work on the R-U-A-Robot dataset (Gros et al., 2021), a dataset containing multiple adversarial ways to ask 'are you a robot' and a medical safety dataset (Abercrombie and Rieser, 2022), a dataset comprised of medical queries annotated by expert practitioners. We found that the semantically informed filters capture not only the input, but also a large set of perturbations and adversarial attacks, allowing for robust representation in safety critical contexts. In the future we plan to focus on how to apply such methods to consider the sequentiality of dialogue, as initially asking the query 'are you a robot', may not have guarantees on subsequent followup query (i.e. 'no seriously?').

### 1.2 Anthropomorphism: What is the balance between naturalness and safety?

While a common goal of AI is to work towards more human-like (anthropomorphic) agents, research should also explore the trade-off between the naturalness of a system and safety of its deployment. Consider Google Duplex (Leviathan and Matias, 2018); a Text-to-Speech (TTS) system for accomplishing real world tasks over the phone. The *inclusion of spontaneous speech phenomena* (such as hesitations) led to highly natural sounding generated responses. However, these responses convinced the human recipients that they were conversing with another human, and also recieved widespread criticism (Lieu, 2018).

This illusion of agency can have harmful consequences when considering safety in conversational AI. NLP researchers have begun to investigate factors that induce personification and develop resources to mitigate such effects. However these efforts are fragmented, and many aspects of anthropomorphism are yet to be considered. Thus in recent work (Abercrombie et al., 2023), we discussed the linguistic factors that contribute to the anthropomorphism of dialogue systems (in Dinkar et al. (2023) with a focus on spontaneous speech phenomena), the harms that can arise, and the recommendations that designers should consider for the development, release, and descriptions of dialogue systems.

## 2 Spoken dialogue system (SDS) research

With chatbot style systems being widely deployed, there needs to be emergent research on safety and robustness, but focusing on real world contexts and the nature of dialogues, rather than (brittle) performance on carefully curated datasets. Ethically, more research needs to be done on the core set of communicative competencies truly required for different kinds of tasks in a dialogue system, to avoid users unnecessarily personifying and relying on the system.

## 3 Suggested topics for discussion

- Ethics of AI, e.g. (unnecessary) anthropomorphism in chatbots and LLMs
- Privacy concerns and data protection, e.g. when adding an LLM to an embodied robot, it not only involves collecting speech/text based inputs, but potentially using video surveillance to analyse input.
- Governance of AI, e.g. how can we create standards that publicly deployed chatbots need to meet (such as, via unit testing)?

## References


Gavin Abercrombie, Amanda Cercas Curry, Tanvi Dinkar, and Zeerak Talat. 2023. Mirages: On anthropomorphism in dialogue systems.

Gavin Abercrombie and Verena Rieser. 2022. Risk-graded safety for handling medical queries in conversational ai. In *Proceedings of the 2nd Conference of the Asia-Pacific Chapter of the Association for Computational Linguistics and the 12th International Joint Conference on Natural Language Processing*. pages 234–243.

Emily M Bender, Timnit Gebru, Angelina McMillan-Major, and Shmargaret Shmitchell. 2021. On the dangers of stochastic parrots: Can language models be too big? In *Proceedings of the 2021 ACM Conference on Fairness, Accountability, and Transparency*. pages 610–623.

A Stevie Bergman, Gavin Abercrombie, Shannon L Spruit, Dirk Hovy, Emily Dinan, Y-Lan Boureau, and Verena Rieser. 2022. Guiding the release of safer e2e conversational ai through value sensitive design. In *Proceedings of the 23rd Annual Meeting of the Special Interest Group on Discourse and Dialogue*. pages 39–52.

Rishi Bommasani, Drew A. Hudson, Ehsan Adeli, Russ Altman, Simran Arora, Sydney von Arx, Michael S. Bernstein, Jeannette Bohg, Antoine Bosselut, Emma Brunskill, Erik Brynjolfsson, Shyamal Buch, Dallas Card, Rodrigo Castellon, Niladri S. Chatterji, Annie S. Chen, Kathleen Creel, Jared Quincy Davis, Dorottya Demszky, Chris Donahue, Moussa Doumbouya, Esin Durmus, Stefano Ermon, John Etchemendy, Kawin Ethayarajh, Li Fei-Fei, Chelsea Finn, Trevor Gale, Lauren Gillespie, Karan Goel, Noah D. Goodman, Shelby Grossman, Neel Guha, Tatsunori Hashimoto,

Peter Henderson, John Hewitt, Daniel E. Ho, Jenny Hong, Kyle Hsu, Jing Huang, Thomas Icard, Saahil Jain, Dan Jurafsky, Pratyusha Kalluri, Siddharth Karamcheti, Geoff Keeling, Fereshte Khani, Omar Khattab, Pang Wei Koh, Mark S. Krass, Ranjay Krishna, Rohith Kuditipudi, and et al. 2021. On the opportunities and risks of foundation models. *CoRR* abs/2108.07258. https://arxiv.org/abs/2108.07258.

Jacob Devlin, Ming-Wei Chang, Kenton Lee, and Kristina Toutanova. 2019. BERT: Pre-Training of Deep Bidirectional Transformers for Language Understanding. In *Proceedings of the 2019 Conference of the North American Chapter of the Association for Computational Linguistics: Human Language Technologies, Volume 1 (Long and Short Papers)*. Association for Computational Linguistics, Minneapolis, Minnesota, pages 4171–4186. https://doi.org/10.18653/v1/N19-1423.

Emily Dinan, Gavin Abercrombie, A. Bergman, Shannon Spruit, Dirk Hovy, Y-Lan Boureau, and Verena Rieser. 2022a. SafetyKit: First aid for measuring safety in open-domain conversational systems. In *Proceedings of the 60th Annual Meeting of the Association for Computational Linguistics (Volume 1: Long Papers)*. Association for Computational Linguistics, Dublin, Ireland, pages 4113–4133. https://doi.org/10.18653/v1/2022.acl-long.284.

Emily Dinan, Gavin Abercrombie, A Bergman, Shannon L Spruit, Dirk Hovy, Y-Lan Boureau, and Verena Rieser. 2022b. Safetykit: First aid for measuring safety in open-domain conversational systems. In *Proceedings of the 60th Annual Meeting of the Association for Computational Linguistics (Volume 1: Long Papers)*. pages 4113–4133.

Tanvi Dinkar, Chloé Clavel, and Ioana Vasilescu. 2023. Fillers in spoken language understanding: Computational and psycholinguistic perspectives. *Traitement Automatique des Langues* 63(3).

Tanvi Dinkar, Pierre Colombo, Matthieu Labeau, and Chloé Clavel. 2020. The importance of fillers for text representations of speech transcripts. In *Proceedings of the 2020 Conference on Empirical Methods in Natural Language Processing (EMNLP)*. Association for Computational Linguistics, Online, pages 7985–7993. https://doi.org/10.18653/v1/2020.emnlp-main.641.

David Gros, Yu Li, and Zhou Yu. 2021. The R-U-A-Robot dataset: Helping avoid chatbot deception by detecting user questions about human or non-human identity.

Di Jin, Zhijing Jin, Joey Tianyi Zhou, and Peter Szolovits. 2019. Is bert really robust? natural language attack on text classification and entailment. *arXiv preprint arXiv:1907.11932* .

California State Legislature. 2018. California senate bill no. 1001.

Yaniv Leviathan and Yossi Matias. 2018. Google duplex: An AI system for accomplishing real world tasks over the phone. *Google AI Blog* .

Johnny Lieu. 2018. Google's creepy AI phone call feature will disclose it's a robot, after backlash. `https://mashable.com/2018/05/11/google-duplex-disclosures-robot`. Mashable. Accessed 2023-03-16.

Christina Montgomery. 2023. Hearing on "Oversight of AI: Rules for Artificial Intelligence". `https://www.ibm.com/policy/wp-content/uploads/2023/05/Christina-Montgomery-Senate-Judiciary-Testimony-5-16-23.pdf`. Accessed: 2023-06-01.

Milad Moradi and Matthias Samwald. 2021. Evaluating the robustness of neural language models to input perturbations. In *Proceedings of the 2021 Conference on Empirical Methods in Natural Language Processing*. Association for Computational Linguistics, Online and Punta Cana, Dominican Republic, pages 1558–1570. https://doi.org/10.18653/v1/2021.emnlp-main.117.

Priyanka Sen. 2020. Speech disfluencies occur at higher perplexities. In *Proceedings of the Workshop on the Cognitive Aspects of the Lexicon*. Association for Computational Linguistics, Online, pages 92–97. https://aclanthology.org/2020.cogalex-1.11.

Laura Weidinger, John Mellor, Maribeth Rauh, Conor Griffin, Jonathan Uesato, Po-Sen Huang, Myra Cheng, Mia Glaese, Borja Balle, Atoosa Kasirzadeh, Zac Kenton, Sasha Brown, Will Hawkins, Tom Stepleton, Courtney Biles, Abeba Birhane, Julia Haas, Laura Rimell, Lisa Anne Hendricks, William Isaac, Sean Legassick, Geoffrey Irving, and Iason Gabriel. 2021. Ethical and social risks of harm from language models.

Tongshuang Wu, Marco Tulio Ribeiro, Jeffrey Heer, and Daniel S Weld. 2021. Polyjuice: Generating counterfactuals for explaining, evaluating, and improving models. *arXiv preprint arXiv:2101.00288* .

Chloe Xiang. 2023. 'He Would Still Be Here': Man Dies by Suicide After Talking with AI Chatbot, Widow Says. `https://www.vice.com/en/article/pkadgm/man-dies-by-suicide-after-talking-with-ai-chatbot-widow-says`. VICE. Accessed: 2023-06-12.

## Biographical sketch

Tanvi Dinkar is a Research Associate at Heriot Watt University, working on Safety in Conversational AI with Prof. Oliver Lemon. She completed her PhD at Télécom Paris, supervised by Prof. Chloé Clavel, Prof. Catherine Pelachaud and Prof. Ioana Vasilescu. Her PhD studied the representations of disfluencies for SLU, and how they can be informative signals of communication, rather than simply removed as noise. During her PhD, she was a Marie Curie Early Stage Researcher at ANIMATAS. Her research interests include safety and robustness in conversational AI, spoken language understanding, how NLP models are brittle compared to real-world dialogues, communicative strategies and pragmatics. Prior to this, she was a dialogue engineer at Nuance (now Microsoft), coding dialogue systems for the automotive industry. She decided to pursue research when she saw from customer tickets that the task oriented dialogue systems are not robust to people speaking naturally. She has two masters from the University of Edinburgh, one in Linguistics and one in Speech and Language Processing. Once upon a time, she completed an undergraduate degree in Journalism and Literature.

**Angus Addlesee**

Heriot-Watt University
Edinburgh, UK

a.addlesee@hw.ac.uk
addlesee.co.uk

## 1 Research interests

Speech production is nuanced and unique to every individual, but today's Spoken Dialogue Systems (SDSs) are trained to use general speech patterns to successfully improve performance on various evaluation metrics. However, these patterns do not apply to certain user groups - often the very people that can benefit the most from SDSs. For example, people with dementia produce more disfluent speech than the general population (Boschi et al., 2017). The healthcare domain is now a popular setting for spoken dialogue and human-robot interaction research. This trend is similar when observing company behaviour. Charities promote industry voice assistants, the creators are getting HIPAA compliance, and their features sometimes target vulnerable user groups (Addlesee, 2023).

### 1.1 Data collection

Research on interactions between SDSs and people with dementia is stifled due to the severe lack of data (Addlesee et al., 2019). Collecting natural spoken dialogue data with vulnerable older adults is ethically challenging. Consent must be witnessed by the participant's carer, the collection location must be designed to be accessible, and collaboration with charities is often required to recruit participants (Addlesee and Albert, 2020). Bespoke tools are also required to collect data *securely* from vulnerable participants (Addlesee, 2022).

In order to tackle this challenge, we have collected two corpora of people with dementia interacting with SDSs. The first corpus, called DEICTIC, contains interactions captured between Amazon Alexa devices and family members in 10 family homes. One member in each family was diagnosed with dementia. This corpus is currently being filtered for personally identifiable information, so its exact size is unknown, but we expect to include over 300 interactions (including both multi-turn and multi-party interactions). Once complete, a sub-repository of TalkBank called DementiaBank[1] will be used to share data with other researchers studying communication in the dementia domain.

The second corpus, yet to be named, is currently being collected as part of the H2020 SPRING Project[2]. We noticed in DEICTIC that multi-party interactions take place at home, even though the system is only designed to have dyadic interactions. Hospital staff that work in a memory clinic also explained that patients typically attend their appointments with a companion. We designed a data collection framework to elicit a diverse range of multi-party conversations between patients, their companions, and a social robot called ARI (Addlesee et al., 2023). We have collected over 50 multi-party conversations with various versions of ARI (with a wizard-of-Oz setup, with a single user system, and with a multi-user system).

| | |
|---|---|
| User: | EVA, Is Alex Rodriguez dating... |
| EVA: | Sorry, I didn't catch that. Dating who? |
| User: | Jennifer Lopez |
| EVA: | Yes, they are currently dating. |

Table 1: Collaborative completion from understanding.

### 1.2 Mid-utterance interruption recovery

Voice assistants interrupt people when they pause mid-utterance, a frustrating interaction that requires the full repetition of the entire sentence again. This impacts all users, but particularly people with cognitive impairments (Boschi et al., 2017). We know, however, that natural spoken language unfolds over time. Our interlocutors process each token as it is uttered, maintaining a partial representation of what has been said (Marslen-Wilson, 1973; Madureira and Schlangen, 2020; Kahardipraja et al., 2021). That is, we understand the words that *were already said* if someone pauses mid-sentence. To avoid waiting indefinitely while a conversation partner is pausing, humans either prompt the turn-holder to collaboratively complete the question (Ginzburg and Sag, 2000; Fernández et al., 2007; Poesio and Rieser, 2010), as shown in Table 1, or suggest sentence completions themselves (referred to as cross-person compound contributions or gap-fillers (Purver et al., 2003; Howes et al., 2011, 2012)), shown in Table 2.

We implemented both approaches to answer people's incomplete questions and semantically parse their disrupted sentences. We constructed two novel cor-

[1] https://dementia.talkbank.org/

[2] https://spring-h2020.eu/



*Proceedings of the 19th Annual Meeting of the Young Reseachers' Roundtable on Spoken Dialogue Systems*, pages 9–11
September 11–12, 2023. 

| | |
|---|---|
| User: | EVA, when is the next solar... |
| EVA: | The next solar eclipse is on the 20th April 2023 |

Table 2: Prediction of question completion.

pora to measure a recovery pipeline's ability to complete these tasks. One corpus interrupts questions originally collected for Knowledge Base Question Answering (KBQA), where a semantic parser is used to convert questions into an executable meaning representation over some given knowledge. For example, a system may be asked to answer "What is the population of Portugal?" when given Wikipedia as a knowledge base. Both the questions and their semantic representations (in SPARQL, a knowledge graph query language) were interrupted, resulting in a corpus of 21,000 interrupted questions (see Tables 1 and 2) (Addlesee and Damonte, 2023a). The second corpus was generated by disrupting almost 80,000 sentences more generally, along with their abstract meaning representations (AMR) (Addlesee and Damonte, 2023b).

We used the current state-of-the-art systems on the corresponding original tasks, given the full original utterances, as performance upper bounds. Our best-performing systems performed remarkably well, identifying where the missing information is located in the utterance's semantic representation. In the KBQA domain, our best pipeline answered only 0.77% fewer questions than the SotA upper bound (Addlesee and Damonte, 2023a). When inspecting sentences more generally, our recovery pipeline lost only 1.6% graph similarity f-score (Smatch) compared to the AMR upper bound (Addlesee and Damonte, 2023b). We have therefore shown that interruption recovery pipelines could potentially be used to improve voice assistant accessibility, and general robustness to noisy environments like family homes, or public spaces (like hospital waiting rooms).

To confirm that our pipelines do improve accessibility in practice, a user study must take place. We have shown that our approach is feasible, but response generation would also be needed for an actual user study. We plan to use our interrupted corpora to elicit clarifications from humans. We can then evaluate whether today's LLMs can safely generate clarification requests to elicit the repair turn from the user.

### 1.3 Real-time semantic parsing

Our incremental semantic parsers in Section 1.2 work when given sentences interrupted at a single point before named entities (where mid-sentence pauses typically occur (Croisile et al., 1996; Seifart et al., 2018; Slegers et al., 2018)), but the next generation of SDSs need to process tokens in real-time (Addlesee and Eshghi, 2021). We have developed a fully incremental graph-based semantic parser by combining Dynamic Syntax (Kempson et al., 2001; Cann et al., 2005) with RDF (Lassila et al., 1998) – called DS-RDF (Addlesee and Eshghi, 2021). A prototype was built[3], but we have since extended the lexicon to be wider coverage. We are also working on an LLM-based approach. We plan to evaluate both of these approaches on our collected corpora. We expect to find that the LLM-based approach has a wider-coverage, but that DS-RDF does not hallucinate as frequently. This is particularly crucial when interacting with vulnerable users in a hospital setting (Addlesee, 2023).

## 2 Spoken dialogue system (SDS) research

The next generation of SDSs need to: (1) process language *incrementally*, token-by-token to be more responsive and enable handling of conversational phenomena; (2) *reason incrementally* allowing meaning to be established beyond what is said; and (3) be *transparent* and *controllable*, allowing designers as well as the system itself to easily establish reasons for particular behaviour and tailor to particular user groups, or domains. The boom of chatGPT (and co) is extremely exciting, but point 3 is a huge concern. Both startups and big tech companies are applying these new approaches to every domain they can, including healthcare. A disastrous news story seems inevitable when one of these systems provides a vulnerable user with a harmful response (e.g. a child, or person with a cognitive impairment). I think the controllability of these systems will be a huge focus for SDS researchers over the next few years.

## 3 Suggested topics for discussion

- Real-time time speech processing
- Multi-party dialogue
- Ethical Data Collection
- LLM controllability and grounding

## Biographical sketch

Angus is currently studying his PhD in Artificial Intelligence at Heriot-Watt University. He has previously worked on machine learning and data science projects within The NHS, Scottish Government, and private clients in many sectors including finance. Angus is very passionate about 'AI for Good', hence his decision to move back into research from industry. He also enjoys bouldering and running.

[3]https://youtu.be/nj-eaMDeEtc?t=903

## References


Angus Addlesee. 2022. Securely capturing people's interactions with voice assistants at home: A bespoke tool for ethical data collection. In *Proceedings of the 2022 NLP for Positive Impact Workshop at EMNLP*.

Angus Addlesee. 2023. Voice assistant accessibility. In *Proceedings of The 13th International Workshop on Spoken Dialogue Systems (IWSDS)*.

Angus Addlesee and Pierre Albert. 2020. Ethically collecting multi-modal spontaneous conversations with people that have cognitive impairments. In *LREC 2020 Workshop Language Resources and Evaluation Conference 11–16 May 2020*. page 15.

Angus Addlesee and Marco Damonte. 2023a. Understanding and answering incomplete questions. In *Proceedings of the 5th Conference on Conversational User Interfaces*.

Angus Addlesee and Marco Damonte. 2023b. Understanding disrupted sentences using underspecified abstract meaning representation. In *Interspeech*.

Angus Addlesee and Arash Eshghi. 2021. Incremental graph-based semantics and reasoning for conversational ai. In *Proceedings of the Reasoning and Interaction Conference (ReInAct 2021)*. pages 1–7.

Angus Addlesee, Arash Eshghi, and Ioannis Konstas. 2019. Current challenges in spoken dialogue systems and why they are critical for those living with dementia. *Dialog for Good (DiGo* .

Angus Addlesee, Weronika Sieińska, Nancie Gunson, Daniel Hernández García, Christian Dondrup, and Oliver Lemon. 2023. Data collection for multi-party task-based dialogue in social robotics. In *The International Workshop on Spoken Dialogue Systems Technology, IWSDS 2023*.

Veronica Boschi, Eleonora Catricala, Monica Consonni, Cristiano Chesi, Andrea Moro, and Stefano F Cappa. 2017. Connected speech in neurodegenerative language disorders: a review. *Frontiers in psychology* 8:269.

Ronnie Cann, Ruth Kempson, and Lutz Marten. 2005. *The Dynamics of Language*. Elsevier, Oxford.

Bernard Croisile, Bernadette Ska, Marie-Josee Brabant, Annick Duchene, Yves Lepage, Gilbert Aimard, and Marc Trillet. 1996. Comparative study of oral and written picture description in patients with alzheimer's disease. *Brain and language* 53(1):1–19.

Raquel Fernández, Jonathan Ginzburg, and Shalom Lappin. 2007. Classifying non-sentential utterances in dialogue: A machine learning approach. *Computational Linguistics* 33(3):397–427.

Jonathan Ginzburg and Ivan Sag. 2000. *Interrogative investigations*. Stanford: CSLI publications.

Christine Howes, Ptarick GT Healey, Matthew Purver, and Arash Eshghi. 2012. Finishing each other's... responding to incomplete contributions in dialogue. In *Proceedings of the Annual Meeting of the Cognitive Science Society*. volume 34.

Christine Howes, Matthew Purver, Patrick GT Healey, Gregory J Mills, and Eleni Gregoromichelaki. 2011. On incrementality in dialogue: Evidence from compound contributions. *Dialogue & Discourse* 2(1):279–311.

Patrick Kahardipraja, Brielen Madureira, and David Schlangen. 2021. Towards incremental transformers: An empirical analysis of transformer models for incremental nlu. *arXiv preprint arXiv:2109.07364* .

Ruth Kempson, Wilfried Meyer-Viol, and Dov Gabbay. 2001. *Dynamic Syntax: The Flow of Language Understanding*. Wiley-Blackwell.

Ora Lassila, Ralph R. Swick, World Wide, and Web Consortium. 1998. Resource description framework (rdf) model and syntax specification .

Brielen Madureira and David Schlangen. 2020. Incremental processing in the age of non-incremental encoders: An empirical assessment of bidirectional models for incremental nlu. *arXiv preprint arXiv:2010.05330* .

William Marslen-Wilson. 1973. Linguistic structure and speech shadowing at very short latencies. *Nature* 244(5417):522–523.

Massimo Poesio and Hannes Rieser. 2010. Completions, coordination, and alignment in dialogue. *Dialogue & Discourse* 1(1).

Matthew Purver, Jonathan Ginzburg, and Patrick Healey. 2003. On the means for clarification in dialogue. In *Current and new directions in discourse and dialogue*, Springer, pages 235–255.

Frank Seifart, Jan Strunk, Swintha Danielsen, Iren Hartmann, Brigitte Pakendorf, Søren Wichmann, Alena Witzlack-Makarevich, Nivja H de Jong, and Balthasar Bickel. 2018. Nouns slow down speech across structurally and culturally diverse languages. *Proceedings of the National Academy of Sciences* 115(22):5720–5725.

Antoine Slegers, Renee-Pier Filiou, Maxime Montembeault, and Simona Maria Brambati. 2018. Connected speech features from picture description in alzheimer's disease: A systematic review. *Journal of Alzheimer's Disease* 65(2):519–542.

**Silvia Colabianchi**

University of Rome La Sapienza
Department of Computer, Control and Management Engineering "Antonio Ruberti"
Via Ariosto 25, 00185, Rome, Italy

silvia.colabianchi@uniroma1.it

## 1 Research Interests

My research interests are in artificial intelligence (AI) and its applications to natural language processing (NLP) and computer vision (CV), with a focus on the **manufacturing sector**. In particular, the research guides practitioners in selecting **architectural and functional elements** for SDSs. A **conceptual architecture** and **taxonomy** were developed (Colabianchi, 2023). The applications developed involve reflections on **slot filling**, **knowledge base (KB)**, and **Large Language Models (LLMs)**.

**Past: a conceptual architecture and a taxonomy**

SDSs represent an intuitive, and innovative solution that is still in the early adopter stage in manufacturing. The research underlined the absence of a reference standard for their logical operation and characteristics. This is also reflected in the literature, in which conflicting statements about the classification criteria and general architecture are often found ((Adamopoulou and Moussiades, 2020; McTear, 2020; Almansor and Hussain, 2020; Souvignier et al., 2000). Thus, from a theoretical point of view, the research composed an architecture that takes into account those developed so far, offering an articulated pathway between the different modules, with details on each step and terminological consistency. The architectural design includes modules from the beginning of the conversation to response generation and interface integration.

From a functional point of view, a taxonomy to support the selection of SDSs elements was developed. Taxonomies are widely recognized in the field of human-computer interaction. They serve a crucial role in enabling the formulation of design principles that can guide the development of future artifacts, such as SDSs. The research readapted the steps suggested by Nickerson et al. (2013). All the iterations integrated reference taxonomies, SDSs literature, and the cross-reading of manufacturing SDSs defining eighteen design dimensions and forty-two characteristics which can be divided into agent and agent-user interaction perspectives. In the first perspective, the taxonomy guides practitioners to ask themselves what objective they want to pursue (e.g., whether to develop a solution for training or to support the operator in complex operations) and how to achieve it (e.g., to include integrations with other tools, to give the chatbot a personification). In the second perspective, the taxonomy guides the choices regarding the type of interaction (e.g., by defining the duration of the conversation or the leader).

The taxonomy revealed important relationships between the dimensions of the design of SDSs for the manufacturing sector, providing interesting insights into their design. The case studies revealed that the rule-based approach is the most widely used, and this is credibly the next frontier that will be surpassed, thanks to the increasing adoption of LLMs (ChatGPT, BARD, etc.) (Li et al., 2022). On the other hand, it will be necessary to leverage generative AI systems toward a narrow knowledge domain, especially in goal-oriented contexts such as industrial applications. The evidence collected reveals a limited propensity for humanization of conversational agents, absence of empathy, and short-lived interaction, highlighting some additional features that current language models (LLMs) can overcome.

**Present: real case applications**

The research continued by testing the results in case studies, highlighting the importance of guiding the organization through the process. SDS applicability for the health and safety of workers was tested (Colabianchi et al., 2022). Next, a task-oriented



*Proceedings of the 19th Annual Meeting of the Young Reseachers' Roundtable on Spoken Dialogue Systems*, pages 12–14
September 11–12, 2023. 

SDS with a slot-filling approach for supporting employees in dealing with complex cybersecurity procedures and cyber threats. Specifically, the SDS was responsible for supporting operators in the attack phase by trying to recover after the attack and limiting the sense of shame felt by users who were victims of phishing attacks (Colabianchi et al., 2023). These applications had some limitations related to the KB and conversation adaptability to the user's profile. They also lacked interaction with external systems, which is increasingly required by industries.

### Future: LLMs and multi-modal applications

The widespread adoption of LLMs represents a significant advancement that can overcome difficulties associated with rule-based and retrieval systems. My research focuses on the use of an SDS as an on-the-job training assistant for a complex assembly task. The solution uses LLM and OpenAI. The results so far are excellent in terms of accuracy of responses, memory, and adaptability of responses to different scenarios. Future work includes improving KB and better speech understanding. Research also investigates the integration of these systems with CV techniques (e.g., for defect identification in production) or integration with Virtual Reality (VR) solutions (e.g., for training production operators in high-risk operations).

## 2 Future of Spoken Dialog Research

I think the future of SDSs research is in extreme personalization. If we think of an SDS to support workers their different qualification has to be considered. A balance must be maintained between conciseness and ease of understanding. The way an experienced user and a novice approach the system can vary, as the novice lacks sufficient knowledge or experience. Additionally, other factors such as specific situations (like emergencies) may also play a role.

In the future also the use of LLMs and related privacy issues should be considered. The use of LLM and external players such as OpenAI frightens the industry. For an optimal KB, it is necessary to provide reports, data, and organizational values for greater customization. Such data sharing with an external player needs to be evaluated in terms of privacy and industry protection.

The third aspect is the evolution of SDSs. What do we expect in the future? How do we envision the integration of these systems with other senses such as sight? How to take into account the need for explainable and interpretable AI?

## 3 Suggestions for discussion

- *The evolution of SDSs: towards a multimodal approach*. Discussion on efficient integration of SDSs with images, videos, or augmented or virtual reality scenarios.
- *Building an optimal knowledge base*. How to work on an optimal KB that takes into account aspects such as:
    - the semantic meaning of words which might vary according to the application context;
    - the continuous update of procedures, reports, and data;
    - the ability to adapt to diction, and dialect, especially in contexts with low schooling personnel.
- *Privacy, industrial protection, and ethics in the era of LLMs and players such as OpenAI.* What conversational systems should and should not know. What are the limits of knowledge? Who is holding it? How to empower industries with deep knowledge of the model.

## References


Eleni Adamopoulou and Lefteris Moussiades. 2020. Chatbots: History, technology, and applications. Machine Learning with Applications, 2:100006.

Ebtesam H. Almansor and Farookh Khadeer Hussain. 2020. Survey on Intelligent Chatbots: State-of-the-Art and Future Research Directions. Advances in Intelligent Systems and Computing, 993:534–543.

Silvia Colabianchi, Margherita Bernabei, and Francesco Costantino. 2022. Chatbot for training and assisting operators in inspecting containers in seaports. Transportation Research Procedia, 64(C):6–13.

Chen Li, Xiaochun Zhang, Dimitrios Chrysostomou, and Hongji Yang. 2022. ToD4IR: A Humanised Task-Oriented Dialogue System for Industrial Robots. IEEE Access.

Colabianchi, S., Tedeschi, A., & Costantino, F. (2023). Human-technology integration with industrial conversational agents: A conceptual architecture and a taxonomy for manufacturing. Journal of Industrial Information Integration, 35, 100510.

Michael McTear. 2020. Conversational AI: Dialogue Systems, Conversational Agents, and Chatbots. Synthesis Lectures on Human Language Technologies, 13(3):1–251.

Robert C. Nickerson, Upkar Varshney, and Jan Muntermann. 2013. A method for taxonomy development and its application in information systems. European Journal of Information Systems, 22(3):336–359.

Bernd Souvignier, Andreas Kellner, Bernhard Rueber, Hauke Schramm, and Frank Seide. 2000. The thoughtful elephant: Strategies for spoken dialog systems. IEEE Transactions on Speech and Audio Processing, 8(1):51–62.

## Biographical Sketch

Silvia Colabianchi is a young research fellow at Sapienza University of Rome. She recently earned a PhD defending a thesis titled "Humans in cyber resilience: managerial and operational opportunities." As part of her thesis, she has undertaken research on SDSs to support employees in managing cybersecurity. She is currently testing her architecture and taxonomy of elements for SDSs. Her research includes the use of a SDS to support operators in alienating and repetitive operations, preserving their creativity and critical thinking. She is currently a member of the task force for the development of Digital Intelligent Assistants for manufacturing established under the COALAH2020 project. Along with this, her future research includes the integration of SDSs with computer vision and virtual reality. In her free time, she enjoys playing padel, tennis, and going hiking in the mountains.

**Biswesh Mohapatra**

INRIA
2 Rue Simone IFF
75012 Paris

biswesh.mohapatra@inria.fr
https://sites.google.com/view/biswesh-mohapatra

## 1 Research interests

**Conversational grounding** is an interactive process that has been studied extensively in cognitive science, whereby participants in a conversation check to make sure their interlocutors understand what is being referred to. (Clark and Brennan, 1991) propose the concept of "common ground" which is the mutual knowledge and mutual assumptions accumulated over the course of a conversation between the interlocutors during this interactive process. This common ground is built via words, of course, but also through the use of other modalities: pointing to objects in the environment, nodding to indicate that one has understood, eye-gaze or varying intonation in the speech, as pointed out by (Nakano et al., 2003). One way of thinking about this is that these units have an **underlying uncertainty** which is negotiated and removed by the participants before getting added to the shared information. The uncertainty comes from ambiguities that could be in the form of spatial references like "that car" or event references like "that was funny". When required, these uncertainties are solved through negotiations by providing additional information from the speaker when they sense a lack of understanding from the listener like "the big one next to the Ferrari" or by the listener themselves by asking for clarifications such as "You mean the blue one?". A grounding mechanism deals with removing the ambiguity between speakers while creating a local common understanding among them. This is important both when the model is the speaker and when it is the listener. Without a good grounding mechanism, conversations would not be robust and would often lead to misunderstandings. In fact, this is evident in the state-of-the-art dialogue systems that are increasingly using **Large Language Models(LLM)** as the Natural Language Understanding and Natural Language Generation modules. These LLMs are incapable of retaining and understanding all the information exchanged with the interlocutor during a session of conversation, as shown by Benotti and Blackburn Benotti and Blackburn (2021). They are also shown to be not very effective at making sure that the listener has grounded the information. Moreover, these LLMs do not have specific architectures to take into consideration the possibility of negotiations, clarifications, or cancellation of information during the conversation. They treat the entire dialog history as one unit where utterances are arranged according to the time. However, many dialogs contain overlapping utterances, and multiple independent pieces of information might be exchanged in parallel, or interleaved. This property of natural spoken dialog makes them unique.

While this process is essential to successful communication between humans and between humans and machines, work needs to be done on testing and building the capabilities of current dialogue systems in managing conversational grounding using the recent progress in LLMs such as Llama (Touvron et al., 2023), Palm (Anil et al., 2023) and GPT4 (OpenAI, 2023). Moreover, these models are text-only models and do not take into consideration the multi-modal aspect of grounding in situated environments. These include non-verbal behaviors, para-verbal behaviors and interaction with the environment. Removing the information present in the intonation of speech can lead to the introduction of ambiguities in the models. For example, an utterance that repeats the previous utterance can either be a confirmation of the previous utterance or a question for clarification depending upon the intonation. Grounding in such a context becomes even more challenging than just text-based models. While text-based large language models are able to take advantage of the vast resources of data available publicly for their training, corpora of multimodal data of daily human interactions are scarce and thus need models with the ability to ground the conversations in such low-resource settings.

Thus my research interests include **testing, understanding, and improving** the functioning of current language models with respect to **Multimodal Conversational Grounding**. My Ph.D. work will build on prior research, in modular dialog systems, that dealt with conversational grounding such as (Traum and Allen, 1994; Paek and Horvitz, 2000). However, since the majority of the previous work has been done using symbolic models that are hard to generalize, the work will take advantage of recent developments in pre-trained LLMs that have shown the ability to generalize to new scenarios.

Specifically, I propose to study and develop a



*Proceedings of the 19th Annual Meeting of the Young Reseachers' Roundtable on Spoken Dialogue Systems*, pages 15–17
September 11–12, 2023. ©2023 Association for Computational Linguistics

framework for incorporating multimodal conversational grounding capabilities into current dialog systems by asking the following questions -

1. How good are current Large Language Models with respect to conversational grounding and where could they be improved?
2. How can multimodal context (for example, a scene that interlocutors are viewing) be inserted into the LLMs to help in conversational grounding?
3. How can we make the models negotiate and align information contained by both participants?
4. How can the grounded information be represented and stored efficiently to use with Large Language Models?

I further elaborate on the above questions and discuss them with respect to the work we are doing, and that we plan to do, in the subsections below.

### 1.1 Testing Capabilities of Dialog Systems

Since, the advent of LLMs, dialog models have been able to take advantage of their capabilities to generate grammatically and semantically correct utterances. However, their performance in phenomena that are specific to dialogs such as conversational grounding has not been studied. We are currently doing a thorough study of the performance of current LLMs like Llama (Touvron et al., 2023) and GPT4 (OpenAI, 2023). Instances from the multi-modal dataset called Meetup (Ilinykh et al., 2019) are used to test the models on different aspects such as disfluencies, ambiguities, and grounding acts like repair, cancellation, acknowledgment, etc.

### 1.2 Incorporating Multimodal Context

Multimodal information coming from non-verbals, paraverbals, and the situated environment are very important for removing ambiguities and building common grounds. Looking at ways to provide such additional context to our language models before processing the dialogs thus becomes very important for a model to successfully ground conversations. The Meetup dataset gives us an opportunity to look into ways to incorporate image context information into LLMs. We also plan to look at other spoken dialogs like Switchboard (Godfrey and Holliman, 1993) to incorporate acoustic information as well.

### 1.3 Negotiating information for Alignment

I am interested in making the model negotiate and align the information contained by the other interlocutor, which is the main purpose of Conversational Grounding. For an effective Spoken Dialog System, we would want the system to ask for a minimum amount of clarifications without compromising on the ability to resolve ambiguities. Hence, the research will look into negotiating common ground by building models that could effectively work with the current LLMs.

### 1.4 Representing and Storing the grounded information

In order to negotiate and ground the information exchanged during a conversation, we need a good and effective way to represent the grounded information for which we might need to remove the ambiguities, that generally come in the form of additional referring expressions where necessary. Additionally, multimodal information from the conversations also may help us to figure out the intents of the utterances which in turn helps us remove ambiguities before storing the grounded information. Exploring ways to store the common ground effectively in order to use it during dialog generation with less inference time is another important topic that the project will look into.

## 2 Spoken dialogue system (SDS) research

It seems clear that spoken dialogue systems(SDS) will start incorporating visual elements as Situated Dialogs become more prominent with the rise of use cases such as Embodied Conversational Agents and Social Robots, in the coming years. I also believe that these agents will begin to serve as Personal Assistants, capable of helping users in learning new skills and also managing their daily schedules. Thus, research in the field of extracting accurate information from users over time and using it effectively would be very important as well. Hence, further work on grounding, including clarifying user communicative intentions through multimodal information, and incorporating world knowledge effectively, will be essential for fulfilling the potential of Spoken Dialog Systems.

## 3 Suggested topics for discussion

- Do we need a different set of architectures for spoken dialog systems that combine the various modalities in better ways or are the current transformer-based models the future?
- How does the advent of models like GPT4 shape the direction of research in Spoken Dialog Systems? What can we learn from these models that can help build better SDS?
- Will an end-to-end dialog system be able to eventually replace modular dialog systems? If not, then what are the key factors that obstruct the current or future end-to-end models from doing so?

## References


Rohan Anil, Andrew M. Dai, Orhan Firat, Melvin Johnson, Dmitry Lepikhin, Alexandre Tachard Passos, Siamak Shakeri, Emanuel Taropa, Paige Bailey, Z. Chen, Eric Chu, J. Clark, Laurent El Shafey, Yanping Huang, Kathleen S. Meier-Hellstern, Gaurav Mishra, Erica Moreira, Mark Omernick, Kevin Robinson, Sebastian Ruder, Yi Tay, Kefan Xiao, Yuanzhong Xu, Yujing Zhang, Gustavo Hernandez Abrego, Junwhan Ahn, Jacob Austin, Paul Barham, Jan A. Botha, James Bradbury, Siddhartha Brahma, Kevin Michael Brooks, Michele Catasta, Yongzhou Cheng, Colin Cherry, Christopher A. Choquette-Choo, Aakanksha Chowdhery, C Crépy, Shachi Dave, Mostafa Dehghani, Sunipa Dev, Jacob Devlin, M. C. D'iaz, Nan Du, Ethan Dyer, Vladimir Feinberg, Fan Feng, Vlad Fienber, Markus Freitag, Xavier García, Sebastian Gehrmann, Lucas González, Guy Gur-Ari, Steven Hand, Hadi Hashemi, Le Hou, Joshua Howland, An Ren Hu, Jeffrey Hui, Jeremy Hurwitz, Michael Isard, Abe Ittycheriah, Matthew Jagielski, Wen Hao Jia, Kathleen Kenealy, Maxim Krikun, Sneha Kudugunta, Chang Lan, Katherine Lee, Benjamin Lee, Eric Li, Mu-Li Li, Wei Li, Yaguang Li, Jun Yu Li, Hyeontaek Lim, Han Lin, Zhong-Zhong Liu, Frederick Liu, Marcello Maggioni, Aroma Mahendru, Joshua Maynez, Vedant Misra, Maysam Moussalem, Zachary Nado, John Nham, Eric Ni, Andrew Nystrom, Alicia Parrish, Marie Pellat, Martin Polacek, Alex Polozov, Reiner Pope, Siyuan Qiao, Emily Reif, Bryan Richter, Parker Riley, Alexandra Ros, Aurko Roy, Brennan Saeta, Rajkumar Samuel, Renee Marie Shelby, Ambrose Slone, Daniel Smilkov, David R. So, Daniela Sohn, Simon Tokumine, Dasha Valter, Vijay Vasudevan, Kiran Vodrahalli, Xuezhi Wang, Pidong Wang, Zirui Wang, Tao Wang, John Wieting, Yuhuai Wu, Ke Xu, Yu Xu, Lin Wu Xue, Pengcheng Yin, Jiahui Yu, Qiaoling Zhang, Steven Zheng, Ce Zheng, Wei Zhou, Denny Zhou, Slav Petrov, and Yonghui Wu. 2023. Palm 2 technical report. *ArXiv* abs/2305.10403.

Luciana Benotti and Patrick Blackburn. 2021. Grounding as a collaborative process. In *Proceedings of the 16th Conference of the European Chapter of the Association for Computational Linguistics: Main Volume*. Association for Computational Linguistics, Online, pages 515–531. https://doi.org/10.18653/v1/2021.eacl-main.41.

Herbert H. Clark and Susan E. Brennan. 1991. Grounding in communication. In Lauren Resnick, Levine B., M. John, Stephanie Teasley, and D., editors, *Perspectives on Socially Shared Cognition*, American Psychological Association, pages 13–1991.

John J. Godfrey and Edward Holliman. 1993. Switchboard-1 release 2 ldc97s62.

Nikolai Ilinykh, Sina Zarrieß, and David Schlangen. 2019. Meet up! a corpus of joint activity dialogues in a visual environment. In *Proceedings of the 23rd Workshop on the Semantics and Pragmatics of Dialogue - Full Papers*. SEMDIAL, London, United Kingdom. http://semdial.org/anthology/Z19-Ilinykh$_{s}emdial_{0}006.pdf$.

Yukiko Nakano, Gabe Reinstein, Tom Stocky, and Justine Cassell. 2003. Towards a model of face-to-face grounding. In *Proceedings of the 41st Annual Meeting of the Association for Computational Linguistics*. Association for Computational Linguistics, Sapporo, Japan, pages 553–561. https://doi.org/10.3115/1075096.1075166.

OpenAI. 2023. Gpt-4 technical report.

Tim Paek and Eric Horvitz. 2000. Conversation as action under uncertainty. In *Proceedings of the Sixteenth Conference on Uncertainty in Artificial Intelligence*. Morgan Kaufmann Publishers Inc., San Francisco, CA, USA, UAI'00, page 455–464.

Hugo Touvron, Thibaut Lavril, Gautier Izacard, Xavier Martinet, Marie-Anne Lachaux, Timothée Lacroix, Baptiste Rozière, Naman Goyal, Eric Hambro, Faisal Azhar, Aur'elien Rodriguez, Armand Joulin, Edouard Grave, and Guillaume Lample. 2023. Llama: Open and efficient foundation language models. *ArXiv* abs/2302.13971.

David Traum and James Allen. 1994. A "speech acts" approach to grounding in conversation .


## Biographical sketch

Biswesh is a PhD student at Inria Paris working with the Articulab group under Prof. Justine Cassell and Prof. Laurent Romary. He did an Integrated Master of Technology majoring in Computer Science and Engineering at IIIT Bangalore, India. During his undergraduate degree he interned at IBM Research AI, Siemens Research and was also a Google Summer of Code Scholar (GSOC) in 2018. During his internship at IBM Research, he was exposed to the field of dialog systems and later worked at Inria for a year as a Research Engineer at Articulab, a group focusing on Multimodal Dialog Systems Research. Prior to his endeavor in research, he co-created an online digital simulator called Circuitverse.org, currently having more than 20,000 users worldwide and has also contributed to open-source platforms like OpenStreetMap.

# Alyssa Allen

The Ohio State University
Oxley Hall
1712 Neil Avenue
Columbus, OH 43210

allen.2334@osu.edu
linguistics.osu.edu/people/allen.2334


## 1 Research interests

My research interests focus on **natural language generation** (NLG) regarding how to make system outputs more intuitive and comprehensible for the human-user and **conversational entrainment and alignment** from the perspective of how dialogue systems could or should personalize its responses to the human user. As it relates to NLG, my current work focuses on training a system to **auto-generate comments** for SQL queries produced by a Text-to-SQL parser. The goal is to make the connection between technical SQL language and the user's question more transparent. My linguistic training lies primarily at the intersection of computational and **sociolinguistics**. As such, my curiosities in conversational entrainment and alignment focus on the extent to which conversational agents can or should adjust their language based on human characteristics such as age, race, gender, etc.

### 1.1 Natural Language Generation (NLG)

My work in natural language generation has revolves around SQL query explainability. Users asking a question to a database may see the query as parsed by the system along with the results. Without notable amounts of training though, SQL commands can be difficult to understand, especially for complex queries. Additionally the output could yield unexpected or misleading results due to an incorrect parse of the user's initial question. The user may not be able to easily identify the mistake if only given the query as explanation.

Past research in making database language more comprehensible to humans have largely taken the route of summary comments or template language (Narechania et al., 2021; Kokkalis et al., 2012; Eleftherakis et al., 2021). These approaches do offer clarity on how the query answers the user's question. That said, templates or summaries can still heavily rely on database terminology (e.g. tables, columns, results, etc) that are not intuitive to the average human. The approaches also do not prioritize infusing user language into the comments or templates, leaving the cognitive load of making these connections to the human.

My research takes the approach of training a system to generate line-by-line comments for each SQL command, avoid database terminology, and leverage the user's language where appropriate. Line-by-line comments can directly state what information is being found in by each SQL command as a step toward answering the user question. One main benefit of this approach is that line-by-line comments can make errors in the SQL query more obvious to the human user.

My ongoing work has been focused on developing training data for such a model. I have manually annotated a small set of user questions and SQL queries. These hand-written examples of ideal comments are being used in few-shot prompting to ChatGPT where the model is tasked with generating comments for unseen queries. This set of ChatGPT-generated comments will become training and dev sets for fine-tuning an open-source LLM.

One challenge to generating natural-sounding comments for incorrect SQL queries is the balance between staying faithful to the query while integrating user language. Current findings suggest ChatGPT favors aligning with user language when the SQL command diverges from the user question, leaving errors hidden. If this bias exists in the ChatGPT-generated comments, it is likely the bias will persist in the fine-tuned open-source LLM as well. Further exploration of how to manage this problem is in progress.

This work will also explore improving the quality of the training and dev sets through filtering and comment refinement strategies. Open-sourced LLMs will be fine-tuned on each version of the training and dev sets to try improving comment generation capabilities. The ultimate goal is to have an open-source LLM be able to auto-generate comments for any unseen query.

### 1.2 Conversational Entrainment and Alignment

As mentioned in the previous section, leveraging the user's language can help alleviate points of confusion when explaining a rigid structure such as a database. Taking the user's language into consideration can also be beneficial in more flexible scenarios with non-database-oriented conversational agents.



*Proceedings of the 19th Annual Meeting of the Young Reseachers' Roundtable on Spoken Dialogue Systems*, pages 18–20
September 11–12, 2023. 

As a future course of research, I am interested in approaching the question of conversational entrainment and alignment with a sociolinguistic lens for task-oriented dialogue systems.

Factors such as age, spoken dialect, relationship, power dynamic, gender, etc all impact human-human conversations. Humans take in this information subconsciously (or at times consciously) and may mirror or distance their language based on judgements made about the second interlocutor. Research in the field of human-machine interactions has started to better understand how humans align with the machine they are speaking to, such as Amazon's Alexa or Apple's Siri (?Cohn et al., 2020), but I am primarily interested in the ways a machine can adjust their speech in order to improve the dialogue experience for humans. Leveraging human-human sociolinguistic findings (e.g. features of child directed speech (Nicola Dawson, 2021), perceptions of humor based on gender (Crawford, 2003), or variation patterns within different communities (Kiesling, 1998; DeCapua et al., 2006; Beebe and Takahashi, 1989) as a basis for future research questions, we can begin to investigate about how those preferences shift or remain intact for human-machine conversations.

My interests in this area build on the Computers Are Social Actors paradigm (Nass et al., 1994). If humans view computers as active interlocutors, then sociolinguistic insights from human-human conversations should provide some guidance in better developing and assessing human-machine conversations.

## 2 Spoken dialogue system (SDS) research

SDS research will continue to dive into questions around interpretability, explainability, and controllability as LLM capabilities progress. Questions around ethical usage of using conversational agents and improving robot social intelligence will also continue to be major considerations in the field. I think a growing interest will be in the dynamics occurring between the human and the dialogue system during a conversation.

As conversational agents become even more commonplace in the coming years, understanding the machine as an active interlocutor will be necessary in order to create more advanced conversational experiences for humans. I am curious about what socially-focused considerations could result in improved levels of personalization versus what adjustments could lead to toxic or harmful speech. For example, one could imagine a dialogue system trained to speak to all women in one way and all men in another would lead to harmful stereotyping. Improved levels of personalization though could take shape as a system picking up on a human user's dialect and leveraging words from that dialect to appear more familiar.

When considering future applications of SDS, it will be crucial for research in academic and industry spaces to be discussed and available between the groups. As products are being developed and launched in industry, findings from academia can be helpful in improving the way these systems are designed. I think this collaboration is where questions around what should a system be capable of in addition to what the system can do will be most effectively addressed.

## 3 Suggested topics for discussion

- What are the potential tradeoffs between developing conversational agents that rely on templated language versus leveraging LLMs to generate more flexible and dynamic dialogue?

- How can sociolinguistic theory impact research on conversational agent entrainment and alignment in order to improve dialogue personalization? How do elements such as the perceived gender of the machine voice impact effectiveness of the dialogue system.

- How can a multi-modal approach reduce cases of conversational ambiguity and improve the human-user experience?

## References


Leslie M. Beebe and Tomoko Takahashi. 1989. *Sociolinguistic Variation in Face-Threatening Speech Acts*, Springer US, Boston, MA, pages 199–218. https://doi.org/10.1007/978-1-4899-0900-8$_1$3.

Michelle Cohn, Patrik Jonell, Taylor Kim, Jonas Beskow, and Georgia Zellou. 2020. Embodiment and gender interact in alignment to tts voices.

Mary Crawford. 2003. Gender and humor in social context. *Journal of Pragmatics* 35(9):1413–1430. The Pragmatics of Humor. https://doi.org/https://doi.org/10.1016/S0378-2166(02)00183-2.

Andrea DeCapua, Diana Berkowitz, and Diana Boxer. 2006. Women talk revisited: Personal disclosures and alignment development 25(4):393–412. https://doi.org/doi:10.1515/MULTI.2006.021.

Stavroula Eleftherakis, Orest Gkini, and Georgia Koutrika. 2021. Let the database talk back: Natural language explanations for sql. In *SEA-Data@VLDB*.

Scott F. Kiesling. 1998. Men's identities and sociolinguistic variation: The case of fraternity men. *Journal of Sociolinguistics* 2:69–99.

Andreas Kokkalis, Panagiotis Vagenas, Alexandros Zervakis, Alkis Simitsis, Georgia Koutrika, and Yannis Ioannidis. 2012. Logos: A system for translating queries into narratives. In *Proceedings of the 2012 ACM SIGMOD International Conference on Management of Data*. Association for Computing Machinery, New York, NY, USA, SIGMOD '12, pages 673–676. https://doi.org/10.1145/2213836.2213929.

Arpit Narechania, Adam Fourney, Bongshin Lee, and Gonzalo Ramos. 2021. Diy: Assessing the correctness of natural language to sql systems. In *26th International Conference on Intelligent User Interfaces*. Association for Computing Machinery, New York, NY, USA, IUI '21, pages 597–607. https://doi.org/10.1145/3397481.3450667.

Clifford Nass, Jonathan Steuer, and Ellen Siminoff. 1994. Computer are social actors. page 204. https://doi.org/10.1145/259963.260288.

Yaling Hsiao Alvin Wei Ming Tan Nilanjana Banerji Kate Nation Nicola Dawson. 2021. Features of lexical richness in children's books: Comparisons with child-directed speech. *Language Development Research, Carnegie Mellon University Library Publishing Service* 1(1).

## Biographical sketch

Alyssa Allen is a second-year PHD student at The Ohio State University. Her work focuses on developing conversational agents that leverage human-user language to generate more natural-sounding conversation turns. She is also interested in pursuing how sociolinguistic insights can improve human-machine communication.

Alyssa has a Master's Degree in Linguistics from Eastern Michigan University and completed her Bachelor's Degree from the University of Michigan. Prior to attending Eastern Michigan University, Alyssa worked in public relations with a focus on helping technology-focused companies promote and explain their AI-driven products to their respective audiences.

**Bram Willemsen**

KTH Royal Institute of Technology
Division of Speech, Music and Hearing
Stockholm, Sweden

bramw@kth.se
willemsenbram.github.io


## 1 Research interests

My current research lies at the intersection of vision and language; more specifically, I am working on problems related to **visually grounded language understanding** for conversational agents. By observing conversations between humans, we aim to improve our understanding of **referring language use in dialogue**, so that we may develop systems capable of engaging in interactions with humans that involve references to a co-observed world.

### 1.1 Referring language use in dialogue

If we define dialogue as an exchange of information, the act of referring can be seen as a speaker attempting to direct the attention of their addressee to some perceivable information of note, i.e. the referent. Participants in a conversation ordinarily collaborate in the process of producing and grounding references (Clark and Wilkes-Gibbs, 1986). Each party may contribute to the description and the successful identification of a referent:

> A: Have you seen my dog?
> B: Golden? Not particularly bright-looking?
> A: No. He is a black Labrador and I'll have you know he's brainier than most people.

Mentions of the same referent in a discourse are said to corefer. For example, in the above exchange *"my dog"* and *"he"* are coreferences, as they denote the same referent.

If we want to model dialogues that reflect this manner of referencing a co-observed world, phenomena such as described should be represented in the data that is used for training and evaluation. Upon review of existing work, we found that few visually-grounded dialogue tasks and datasets had explicitly accounted for these dialogue phenomena. This led us to introduce a task of our own, a collaborative image ranking task we called **A Game Of Sorts** (Willemsen et al., 2022). In this grounded agreement game (Schlangen, 2019), two players are asked to rank nine images based on a given sorting criterion. The game is implemented as a web application that has players exchange text-based messages to discuss how the scenarios with which they are presented–and in which these sorting criteria are embedded–should affect the rank of each image. Although the players see the same images, the position of the images on their screens is randomized. This forces them to refer to each image based on its content rather than its position on screen. We define task success as the players managing to reach an agreement on which rank to assign to each image *and* actually assigning the agreed upon ranks to the same images; the latter is not a given due to the players not being able to see each other's perspective. As the game is played over multiple rounds with the same set of images, we effectively guarantee repeated mentions of the same referents. Analysis of dialogues collected with our task showed it managed to induce mixed-initiative interactions in which the phenomena of interest were present.

### 1.2 Visually grounded language understanding

Recent advances in multimodal representation learning have led to significant improvements on vision-language benchmarks. Vision-language models (VLMs), such as CLIP (Radford et al., 2021), that have been pretrained on hundreds of millions of image-text pairs, learn to jointly embed both modalities via contrastive objectives. The learned representations have shown to be useful for downstream tasks that involve matching images and text.

Nevertheless, we recognize a few limitations of the current paradigm when we consider interactive settings in which pretrained models encounter new information. Incorporating new information in already trained models remains a challenge (see e.g. Parisi et al., 2019). Retraining from scratch in light of new data is currently not a feasible solution due to the resource-intensive nature of the process. Moreover, these VLMs are trained on large image captioning datasets or similar data from web-based sources that contain images paired with (high-level) descriptions. Although models trained on this data learn to associate (visual representations of) things with the words and phrases that are commonly used to describe them, this general language use may not align with how humans in a conversation would describe those same things. Take, for instance, mentions of referents that are non-descriptive in terms of visually perceivable attributes, such as names of pets: no pretrained model can reasonably be assumed to know, *out of the box*, that a particular dog goes by the name of *Sir Gideon Ofnir,*



*Proceedings of the 19th Annual Meeting of the Young Reseachers' Roundtable on Spoken Dialogue Systems*, pages 21–23
September 11–12, 2023. 

*the All-Knowing*. For these reasons, we experimented with rapid domain adaptation based on a simple model that learns to transform VLM embeddings to better align the representations with the expected language use without updating the parameters of the base model (Skantze and Willemsen, 2022). Although this approach does not provide a fundamental solution to continual learning with VLMs, as the newly acquired knowledge is not incorporated into the base model, it does provide an opportunity–albeit limited–to adapt to users during an interaction.

A further challenge is the handling of longer texts. Given that most VLMs have been trained to optimize for matching relatively short, high-level descriptions with their associated images, they do not learn to process discourse-like inputs. This limits their zero-shot performance on tasks that require image-text matching based on conversational inputs. Reference resolution in visually-grounded dialogue, by which we mean the grounding of mentions to their exophoric referents, can be formulated as such a task. We proposed an approach to this task (Willemsen et al., 2023) that addressed the discourse processing limitations of pretrained VLMs by fine-tuning a causal large language model (LLM) to function as an auxiliary discourse processor: the pretrained LLM learns to generate definite descriptions of referents based on the (co)referential information in the dialogue; the generated descriptions are then used by the pretrained VLM for zero-shot identification of referents.

## 2 Spoken dialogue system (SDS) research

In the coming years, I expect much emphasis to be put on learning to integrate modalities end-to-end. Problems that are inherently multimodal, which aside from SDSs also includes visually grounded language understanding, ultimately require solutions that respect the interactions between modalities. For example, even though we can use an automatic speech recognition system to transcribe speech and use an LLM as the natural language understanding component of the SDS to processes the transcription, we would miss out on extralinguistic context, such as the prosodic cues that were present in the speech signal, that may be vital to the interpretation of the message: in trying to understand what message someone is attempting to convey, we do not simply take note of the uttered words; we also pay attention to how those words were uttered.

## 3 Suggested topics for discussion

- Drawbacks of LLMs: What are the potential negative consequences for end users of the unchecked use of LLMs in SDSs?
- Influence from industry: To what extent should corporate interests be allowed to dictate the direction of academic research?
- Governance of AI: How can we expect SDS research to be affected by looming regulations?

## References


Herbert H. Clark and Deanna Wilkes-Gibbs. 1986. Referring as a collaborative process. *Cognition* 22(1):1–39. https://doi.org/10.1016/0010-0277(86)90010-7.

German I. Parisi, Ronald Kemker, Jose L. Part, Christopher Kanan, and Stefan Wermter. 2019. Continual lifelong learning with neural networks: A review. *Neural Networks* 113:54–71. https://doi.org/10.1016/j.neunet.2019.01.012.

Alec Radford, Jong Wook Kim, Chris Hallacy, Aditya Ramesh, Gabriel Goh, Sandhini Agarwal, Girish Sastry, Amanda Askell, Pamela Mishkin, Jack Clark, Gretchen Krueger, and Ilya Sutskever. 2021. Learning Transferable Visual Models From Natural Language Supervision. In Marina Meila and Tong Zhang, editors, *Proceedings of the 38th International Conference on Machine Learning*. PMLR, volume 139 of *Proceedings of Machine Learning Research*, pages 8748–8763. https://proceedings.mlr.press/v139/radford21a.html.

David Schlangen. 2019. Grounded Agreement Games: Emphasizing Conversational Grounding in Visual Dialogue Settings. *CoRR* abs/1908.11279. http://arxiv.org/abs/1908.11279.

Gabriel Skantze and Bram Willemsen. 2022. CoLLIE: Continual Learning of Language Grounding from Language-Image Embeddings. *J. Artif. Int. Res.* 74. Place: El Segundo, CA, USA Publisher: AI Access Foundation. https://doi.org/10.1613/jair.1.13689.

Bram Willemsen, Dmytro Kalpakchi, and Gabriel Skantze. 2022. Collecting Visually-Grounded Dialogue with A Game Of Sorts. In *Proceedings of the Thirteenth Language Resources and Evaluation Conference*. European Language Resources Association, Marseille, France, pages 2257–2268. https://aclanthology.org/2022.lrec-1.242/.

Bram Willemsen, Livia Qian, and Gabriel Skantze. 2023. Resolving references in visually-grounded dialogue via text generation. In *Proceedings of the 24th Meeting of the Special Interest Group on Discourse and Dialogue*. Association for Computational Linguistics, Prague, Czechia, pages 457–469. https://aclanthology.org/2023.sigdial-1.43.


## Biographical sketch

Bram Willemsen is a PhD student at KTH Royal Institute of Technology at the Division of Speech, Music and

Hearing (TMH) working towards visually grounded language understanding for conversational agents in the context of the WASP-funded RoboGround project. Before starting his doctoral studies in Sweden in 2019, he studied and worked at Tilburg University, completing his MSc degree (cum laude) in 2017 and working as a Junior Researcher (full-time) on the Horizon 2020-funded L2TOR project until 2019. He enjoys thought-provoking discussions that induce existential dread and long walks on the beach.

Koji Inoue

Kyoto University, Kyoto, Japan
inoue.koji.3x@kyoto-u.ac.jp
http://www.sap.ist.i.kyoto-u.ac.jp/members/inoue/

## 1 Research interests

The advent of large language models (LLMs) has progressively transformed advanced spoken dialogue systems (SDSs) into a commonplace reality. Expected to be integrated into a wide range of robotics in the future, these systems are poised to be implemented in different societal contexts. The author has heretofore engaged in the realization of several SDSs utilizing android robots (Inoue et al. (2020)). While the functionality of these SDSs has primarily been limited to laboratory settings, future efforts aim to incorporate real-world environments such as hospitals, shopping malls, and schools, thereby exerting a profound societal impact through the advancement of SDS research.

### 1.1 Social SDSs in real field

While LLMs are powerful tools, they are not guaranteed to handle all social tasks in the real world. Moreover, even with appropriate prompt-tuning, the issue of hallucination can be fatal in social tasks. First of all, it is necessary to organize a taxonomy of various social dialogue tasks through different perspectives. The author's research group has categorized social tasks into two axes: the speaking role and the listening role. For instance, situations that predominantly require the speaking role can be such as "information guide," while situations emphasizing the listening role can be such as "attentive listening." The key point is to design multiple dialogue tasks that evenly cover the space created by these two axes.

To achieve socially capable SDSs, numerous technical aspects must be addressed. For example, the systems must be capable of handling longer dialogues and long-term interactions. Specifically, they need to effectively store and refer to past dialogues as well as the attributes of the interlocutors. While LLMs are based on the transformer architecture, it is important to question whether simply extending the prompt length is sufficient. Human memory mechanisms are more efficient and self-organizing, so it may be worthwhile to explore explicit models inspired by human memory for improved performance. Furthermore, there will be a need for functionality that enables the expression and updating of the system's own personality. By achieving the above-mentioned features, the research goal of the author is to establish a relationship between systems and users through social dialogue, fostering rapport and trust.

### 1.2 Robust and smooth turn-taking system

When testing SDSs in real-world scenarios, turn-taking always becomes a critical and primitive issue. Conversational robots often face challenges in effectively acquiring turns, leading to situations where the user ends up speaking continuously without interaction. The systems may interrupt and interject in the middle of the user's speech, even before the user has finished their turns. In human-human dialogue, this is not the case owing to a sophisticated mechanism for adaptation, allowing us to engage in conversations with others for extended periods, even several hours. Consequently, conversing with a robot lacking an appropriate turn-taking system can quickly lead to disengagement.

The author has previously proposed several models for turn-taking systems. However, achieving human-level robustness and smoothness in turn-taking still remains a challenge. Additionally, with the emergence of large pre-trained models such as wav2vec 2.0 and AudioLM, there is growing interest in harnessing these models to develop end-to-end systems. Currently staying at KTH Royal Institute of Technology, the author is actively exploring the potential of turn-taking models utilizing large pre-trained models. The ultimate goal is to deploy such models in real-time conversational robots. The mechanism underlying human turn-taking can be seen as a sophisticated architecture that encompasses not only local language understanding but also global dialogue comprehension, response generation, and so on. Ultimately the author aims to investigate models that incorporate these intricate functionalities into SDSs.

### 1.3 Evaluation method for social SDSs

In the process of practical implementation of SDSs, another crucial aspect is the evaluation methodology. In the field of conversational robots, reliance on subjective evaluations has been common, which poses challenges to research reproducibility and hinders the expansion of the research field. Therefore, efforts are being made to develop objective and effective evaluation metrics. Specifically, the author is working on constructing a framework to indirectly evaluate the "human-likeness" of systems based on users' multimodal behaviors. For example, in human-human dialogues, many interactive backchannels are observed to keep people engaged in the dialogue. Inspired by this, if we observe many backchannels from



*Proceedings of the 19th Annual Meeting of the Young Reseachers' Roundtable on Spoken Dialogue Systems*, pages 24–25
September 11–12, 2023. ©2023 Association for Computational Linguistics

users, it might be said that the system could conduct a conversation in a more human-like manner. The ultimate goal is to empower conversational robots to engage in self-reflection, autonomously learn, and evolve by evaluating their dialogues using objective evaluation metrics.

## 2 Spoken dialogue system (SDS) research

In the upcoming years, SDS research is expected to shift its focus toward practicality. It is crucial to go beyond mere applications and strive for a more human-like understanding and behavior in SDSs. Note that it would potentially need another discussion on whether human-likeness is needed for SDSs.

### 2.1 Deeper mind state of user

To achieve a deeper understanding of users, it is essential to conduct studies that delve beyond the surface level of dialogue and explore the inner states of humans. One aspect of the inner state can be identified as *emotion*. Despite the extensive research conducted on emotion recognition and dialogue modeling based on user emotions, there remains a question of whether current models of emotion recognition can adequately capture the intricacies of emotions within dynamically changing social dialogue contexts. In social dialogue scenarios, more subtle emotions undergo dynamic fluctuations. As humans, we adjust our dialogues from micro to macro levels while interpreting these nuanced emotional changes in our conversation partners. By achieving such capabilities, SDSs can explore the user's deeper inner state and become trusted entities in our society.

Furthermore, advancing research in this field will require interdisciplinary approaches that involve fields such as psychology. Therefore, for young researchers and developers in the SDS field, it is desirable to actively acquire not only engineering knowledge but also insights from the humanities and social sciences.

### 2.2 Relationship with society

Furthermore, for SDSs and conversational robots to truly become social entities, it is necessary for them to engage in not only one-on-one conversations but also in multi-party and multi-session dialogues. However, despite the significance of data-driven approaches in the current era, there is a scarcity of datasets available for learning and simulating such dialogues. Given the unlikelihood of a comprehensive dataset being readily available, it becomes necessary to divide the problem and construct datasets initially for individual issues. For instance, in the context of multi-party dialogues, it is possible to separate the problem into two distinct tasks: multi-party turn-taking prediction and response generation. By repeatedly constructing such datasets and proposing new problem formulations, it becomes essential to solidify the emerging tasks for multi-party SDSs. Furthermore, rather than confining conversations to a single user, it is valuable to aim for situations where information propagates through interactions between the system and multiple users, ultimately fostering a sense of community.

To achieve this, standardization of datasets and experimental systems is necessary. Unlike the presence of a common framework such as ROS (robot operating system) in robotic systems, SDSs often require individual research groups to build their systems from scratch. It would be desirable to develop a common system that includes available datasets to improve this situation.

## 3 Suggested topics for discussion

The author would like to propose the following topics for discussion.

- What practical and societal dialogue tasks can be achieved with LLM in the coming years?
- To what extent can SDSs delve into the user's inner states? Additionally, how can we ensure the accuracy and reproducibility of SDSs?
- What type of relationship between SDSs and users should be considered ideal for advancing research and development? Should SDSs be convenient tools such as other generative AIs, providing surface-level interactions? Or should they aim for a socially engaged relationship, similar to a friend, where personal matters can be shared?

## Acknowledgments

This work was supported by JST ACT-X (JPMJAX2103). The author deeply appreciates the constructive comments and valuable feedback provided by the reviewers.

## References

Koji Inoue et al. 2020. An attentive listening system with android ERICA: Comparison of autonomous and WOZ interactions. In *SIGDIAL*.

## Biographical sketch

Koji Inoue received his Ph.D. from the Graduate School of Informatics, Kyoto University, Japan, in 2018. Currently, he serves as an assistant professor at Kyoto University. Additionally, he is currently a visiting researcher at KTH Royal Institute of Technology, Sweden. He has developed a spoken dialogue system for android ERICA. He is a winner of NETEXPLO Innovation 2022 Award.

**Anouck Braggaar**

Tilburg University
Warandelaan 2
5037 AB Tilburg

A.R.Y.Braggaar@tilburguniversity.edu
https://www.tilburguniversity.edu/staff/a-r-y-braggaar

## 1 Research interests

Many companies use **dialogue systems** for their **customer service**, and although there has been a rise in the usage of these systems (Costello and LoDolce, 2022), many of these systems still face challenges in comprehending and properly responding to the customer (Følstad et al., 2021). In our project[1] we aim to figure out how to develop and improve these conversational agents. Part of this project, focuses on the detection of **breakdown patterns** and the possible solutions (**repairs**) to mitigate negative results of these errors.

### 1.1 Conversational breakdowns

Breakdowns lead to frustration and an overall downgraded customer experience (Ashktorab et al., 2019). Therefore it is important to be able to detect these breakdowns and properly solve them to mitigate these negative effects. One of the important questions to start with when looking at breakdowns is to define what a breakdown actually is and what triggers this breakdown (or taking a different perspective, what happens within conversations without breakdowns?) In the next section I will first discuss the research plan we have to figure out if there are different kinds of breakdowns and eventually in Section 1.2 if we can solve the consequent issues through repairs. In this project we will focus on text-based task-oriented customer service chatbots; incorporating features such as speech will lead to very different breakdowns (for example arising from the ASR part of a system).

Errors are often the cause of leading to a breakdown, which leads to the user not being able to continue the conversation (Higashinaka et al., 2015b). There have been attempts to create taxonomies of errors for open-domain systems (Higashinaka et al., 2015a, 2021). Similar to our project, the work of Reinkemeier and Gnewuch (2022) focuses on a text based dialogue system in a specific domain (in their case an insurance company). They aim to find the causes of conversational breakdowns by conducting a cluster analysis of messages leading to breakdowns. We will follow a similar approach as Reinkemeier and Gnewuch (2022) by trying to cluster utterances and figure out if we can detect reasons for initiating repairs. We use real-life Dutch chatbot data from a railroad company. The conversations cover a diverse range of topics, from asking for a ticket refund to travel directions.

Are there any linguistic patterns to be found in utterances before breakdowns occur? Or are there certain topics the chatbot is not capable of handling? To figure out the potential reasons for breakdowns, we use repairs as a proxy. The advantage of using the railroad chatbot dataset is that it has a fixed set of chatbot initiated repairs. From this set we have selected three general repairs that are used in various situations:

1. Not understanding the user and asking for rephrasing: 'Unfortunately I don't fully understand what you mean. Could you rephrase the question in different words? Tip: I understand short and concise questions the best.'
2. Not being able to help and redirecting to human employee: 'I'm sorry, I believe I can not help you yet. Shall I connect you with my colleague?'
3. Apologising and redirecting to human employee: 'I'm sorry to hear that something isn't to your satisfaction. I can unfortunately not register your complaint, but my colleague from customer support is happy to help. Click on the button below.'

These repairs are used anytime the chatbot is not capable of answering the customer query (the last focuses on complaints but is also used in situations were the customers is slightly negative). Possibly not all breakdowns/miscommunications are caught with this approach (for example when the chatbot answers with an irrelevant answer) but the dataset is too large to manually examine every conversation.

Similar to Reinkemeier and Gnewuch (2022) we will use a clustering approach to figure out if there are patterns to be found in breakdowns. We will add multiple features partly derived from Reinkemeier and Gnewuch (2022) who use for example semantic weight and percentage of unknown words. For example, we will also use the number of sentences, characters, and tokens in an utterance. We also will create more complex features as well. As an example we will make use of commonness as described by Meij et al. (2012). Making use of anchors, this metric scores commonness of n-grams based

[1] https://www.conversationalagentsresearch.com/



*Proceedings of the 19th Annual Meeting of the Young Reseachers' Roundtable on Spoken Dialogue Systems*, pages 26–29
September 11–12, 2023. ©2023 Association for Computational Linguistics

on Wikipedia data. We will combine this score together with training data of the bot. This means that words with high scores for commonness, that are not part of the training data, might indicate a wrong interpretation.

### 1.2 ... and Repairs

Miscommunication is an important concept in human language (see for an extensive discussion for example Healey et al. (2018)), sometimes resulting in breakdowns. It is not always possible to prevent breakdowns, which underscores the importance of repairs. As breakdowns occur in many different situations it is necessary to critically think about the 'best' repair for any given situation. So, after focusing on breakdowns we like to find out how to mitigate these breakdowns by using repairs. As was discussed in Section 1.1 we have used the existing repairs as a proxy to detect breakdowns. We could wonder if these repairs are actually the best repairs to fix a conversational breakdown. Different forms of breakdowns, systems or different user groups might need different repair strategies. Ashktorab et al. (2019) for example discuss that chit-chat systems have different goals with repairs (not repairing but engaging for further conversation).

Repair is an important notion studied in conversation analysis to study problem resolving in conversation. The basis of the notion is explained by Schegloff et al. (1977). The notion of repair is later also applied on dialogue systems as breakdowns in conversation with bots are common. Ashktorab et al. (2019) investigate user preference for eight repair strategies. Some of these strategies occur in commercial systems, others are novel strategies that incorporate some of the inner workings of the algorithms behind the dialogue system. They find that both providing options and giving explanations are preferred by users (Ashktorab et al., 2019). Bohus and Rudnicky (2005) focus on non-understanding errors and recovery strategies in spoken systems. They compare the recovery strategies and also investigate how the user responds to these strategies. A different approach is taken by Cuadra et al. (2021) who investigate the self repair of a spoken system (Amazon Alexa) and how it affects the interaction. They show that if an error occurs, a repair is appreciated but when no error occurs a repair can worsen the experience. Lastly, Skantze (2005) examine how humans recover from speech recogniser errors by corrupting speech output. These errors will be similar in spoken dialogue systems. They show that if participants face speech recognition errors, they will ask task-related questions.

## 2 Spoken dialogue system (SDS) research

Since my submission last year, much has changed within the field of dialogue systems. With the advent of ChatGPT and subsequent open alternatives (such as Alpaca (Taori et al., 2023) and Open Assistant), there has been renewed (media)attention for dialogue systems and chatbots. These new technologies will bring new possibilities for research into dialogue systems but also new challenges. I suspect that much more research will focus on the challenges and problems these systems will bring, in for example the context of education (Kasneci et al., 2023) and hospitality (Gursoy et al., 2023). I also suspect that the (general) public gets more and more familiar with these systems and the (assumed) capabilities of systems like chatGPT. Due to both positive and negative attention to these technologies, expectations of the public towards dialogue systems will also shift. Therefore it seems important to learn more about expectations of users and the ways in which we can manage those expectations. Previous research has already shown that expectation management is an important factor. For a chatbot to be successful the user needs to know what to expect from the beginning (Brandtzaeg and Følstad, 2018). Previous work has also stressed the importance of understanding the user perceptions and expectations before building the chatbot (Zamora, 2017), and creating chatbots with characteristics that are in line with users' expectations (Chaves and Gerosa, 2021). Users tend to evaluate chatbots worse when the experience does not line up with their expectations (de Sá Siqueira et al., 2023). Similar research is now also done with chatGPT, for example surveying the expectations of healthcare workers on adopting chatGPT in their work (Temsah et al., 2023).

## 3 Suggested topics for discussion

**Breakdowns and repairs** Can we mitigate negative effects after encountering erroneous chatbots with only repairs or are there other solutions as well? Should we tailor repairs to specific situations or breakdowns?

**Cooperate with industry** In what way can academia cooperate with industry and how far should we go to make our research usable directly for industry? For which purposes can our research be used in the industry? Research has already shown that big tech companies shape research to cater to their needs (Whittaker, 2021; Abdalla and Abdalla, 2021), having its influence grow over the last few years (Abdalla et al., 2023).

**Incorporating ChatGPT** What are the issues with incorporating current technologies like ChatGPT in dialogue systems for both research and industry? Can we overcome issues with interpretability, transparency and replicability? How should we evaluate closed models if we don't know what is exactly in the training data (Rogers et al., 2023)? Should our focus be on the more open models such as Stanford Alpaca (Taori et al., 2023)?

## Acknowledgements

This project has been funded by the NWO Smooth Operators project (KIVI.2019.009).

## References


Mohamed Abdalla and Moustafa Abdalla. 2021. The grey hoodie project: Big tobacco, big tech, and the threat on academic integrity. In *Proceedings of the 2021 AAAI/ACM Conference on AI, Ethics, and Society*. pages 287–297.

Mohamed Abdalla, Jan Philip Wahle, Terry Ruas, Aurélie Névéol, Fanny Ducel, Saif M Mohammad, and Karën Fort. 2023. The elephant in the room: Analyzing the presence of big tech in natural language processing research. In *61st Annual Meeting of the Association for Computational Linguistics*.

Zahra Ashktorab, Mohit Jain, Q Vera Liao, and Justin D Weisz. 2019. Resilient chatbots: Repair strategy preferences for conversational breakdowns. In *Proceedings of the 2019 CHI conference on human factors in computing systems*. pages 1–12.

Dan Bohus and Alexander I. Rudnicky. 2005. Sorry and I didn't catch that! - an investigation of non-understanding errors and recovery strategies. In *Proceedings of the 6th SIGdial Workshop on Discourse and Dialogue*. Special Interest Group on Discourse and Dialogue (SIGdial), Lisbon, Portugal, pages 128–143. https://aclanthology.org/2005.sigdial-1.14.

Petter Bae Brandtzaeg and Asbjørn Følstad. 2018. Chatbots: changing user needs and motivations. *interactions* 25(5):38–43.

Ana Paula Chaves and Marco Aurelio Gerosa. 2021. How should my chatbot interact? A survey on social characteristics in human–chatbot interaction design. *International Journal of Human–Computer Interaction* 37(8):729–758.

Katie Costello and Matt LoDolce. 2022. Gartner predicts chatbots will become a primary customer service channel within five years. [Accessed June 14, 2023]. https://www.gartner.com/en/newsroom/press-releases/2022-07-27-gartner-predicts-chatbots-will-become-a-primary-customer-service-channel-within-five-years.

Andrea Cuadra, Shuran Li, Hansol Lee, Jason Cho, and Wendy Ju. 2021. My bad! Repairing intelligent voice assistant errors improves interaction. *Proceedings of the ACM on Human-Computer Interaction* 5(CSCW1):1–24.

Marianna A de Sá Siqueira, Barbara CN Müller, and Tibor Bosse. 2023. When do we accept mistakes from chatbots? The impact of human-like communication on user experience in chatbots that make mistakes. *International Journal of Human–Computer Interaction* pages 1–11.

Asbjørn Følstad, Theo Araujo, Effie Lai-Chong Law, Petter Bae Brandtzaeg, Symeon Papadopoulos, Lea Reis, Marcos Baez, Guy Laban, Patrick McAllister, Carolin Ischen, et al. 2021. Future directions for chatbot research: an interdisciplinary research agenda. *Computing* 103(12):2915–2942.

Dogan Gursoy, Yu Li, and Hakjun Song. 2023. Chatgpt and the hospitality and tourism industry: an overview of current trends and future research directions. *Journal of Hospitality Marketing & Management* pages 1–14.

Patrick G. T. Healey, Jan P. de Ruiter, and Gregory J. Mills. 2018. Editors' introduction: Miscommunication. *Topics in Cognitive Science* 10(2):264–278. https://doi.org/https://doi.org/10.1111/tops.12340.

Ryuichiro Higashinaka, Masahiro Araki, Hiroshi Tsukahara, and Masahiro Mizukami. 2021. Integrated taxonomy of errors in chat-oriented dialogue systems. In *Proceedings of the 22nd Annual Meeting of the Special Interest Group on Discourse and Dialogue*. pages 89–98.

Ryuichiro Higashinaka, Kotaro Funakoshi, Masahiro Araki, Hiroshi Tsukahara, Yuka Kobayashi, and Masahiro Mizukami. 2015a. Towards taxonomy of errors in chat-oriented dialogue systems. In *Proceedings of the 16th Annual Meeting of the Special Interest Group on Discourse and Dialogue*. Association for Computational Linguistics, Prague, Czech Republic, pages 87–95. https://doi.org/10.18653/v1/W15-4611.

Ryuichiro Higashinaka, Masahiro Mizukami, Kotaro Funakoshi, Masahiro Araki, Hiroshi Tsukahara, and Yuka Kobayashi. 2015b. Fatal or not? Finding errors that lead to dialogue breakdowns in chat-oriented dialogue systems. In *Proceedings of the 2015 Conference on Empirical Methods in Natural Language Processing*. Association for Computational Linguistics, Lisbon, Portugal, pages 2243–2248. https://doi.org/10.18653/v1/D15-1268.

Enkelejda Kasneci, Kathrin Seßler, Stefan Küchemann, Maria Bannert, Daryna Dementieva, Frank Fischer, Urs Gasser, Georg Groh, Stephan Günnemann, Eyke Hüllermeier, et al. 2023. Chatgpt for good? On opportunities and challenges of large language models for education. *Learning and Individual Differences* 103:102274.

Edgar Meij, Wouter Weerkamp, and Maarten De Rijke. 2012. Adding semantics to microblog posts. In *Proceedings of the fifth ACM international conference on Web search and data mining*. pages 563–572.

Fabian Reinkemeier and Ulrich Gnewuch. 2022. Designing effective conversational repair strategies for chatbots. In *Proceedings of the 30th European Conference on Information Systems (ECIS 2022)*.

Anna Rogers, Niranjan Balasubramanian, Leon Derczynski, Jesse Dodge, Alexander Koller, Sasha Luccioni, Maarten Sap, Roy Schwartz, Noah A. Smith, and Emma Strubell. 2023. Closed ai models make bad baselines. https://hackingsemantics.xyz/2023/closed-baselines/.

Emanuel A Schegloff, Gail Jefferson, and Harvey Sacks. 1977. The preference for self-correction in the organization of repair in conversation. *Language* 53(2):361–382.

Gabriel Skantze. 2005. Exploring human error recovery strategies: Implications for spoken dialogue systems. *Speech Communication* 45(3):325–341.

Rohan Taori, Ishaan Gulrajani, Tianyi Zhang, Yann Dubois, Xuechen Li, Carlos Guestrin, Percy Liang, and Tatsunori B Hashimoto. 2023. Alpaca: A strong, replicable instruction-following model. *Stanford Center for Research on Foundation Models. https://crfm. stanford. edu/2023/03/13/alpaca. html* 3(6):7.

Mohamad-Hani Temsah, Fadi Aljamaan, Khalid H Malki, Khalid Alhasan, Ibraheem Altamimi, Razan Aljarbou, Faisal Bazuhair, Abdulmajeed Alsubaihin, Naif Abdulmajeed, Fatimah S Alshahrani, et al. 2023. Chatgpt and the future of digital health: A study on healthcare workers' perceptions and expectations. In *Healthcare*. MDPI, volume 11, page 1812.

Meredith Whittaker. 2021. The steep cost of capture. *Interactions* 28(6):50–55.

Jennifer Zamora. 2017. I'm sorry, dave, i'm afraid i can't do that: Chatbot perception and expectations. In *Proceedings of the 5th international conference on human agent interaction*. pages 253–260.

## Biographical sketch

Anouck Braggaar is a second year PhD candidate at Tilburg University. Her work focuses on conversational agents for customer service and is part of the Smooth Operators project[1]. Currently she is working on a literature review on evaluation approaches for task-oriented dialogue systems and on a study to automatically detect reasons for repair. Previously, she received a research master in Linguistics at the University of Groningen.

# Armand Stricker

Université Paris-Saclay, CNRS, Laboratoire Interdisciplinaire des Sciences du Numérique
91400, Orsay, France
armand.stricker@lisn.upsaclay.fr


## 1 Research interests

My research interests lie at the **intersection between chitchat and task-oriented dialogues** (TODs), with a specific focus on **integrating capabilities typically associated with chitchat systems into task-oriented agents**. In the SDS literature, these two modes of communication are commonly depicted with a clear contrast. On the one hand, chitchat dialogues are characterized as open-domain and usually involve a wide range of topics; chitchat agents are expected to embody all the qualities of an ideal conversationalist and be empathetic, engaging, knowledgeable, and well-behaved. On the other hand, TODs are closed-domain and rely on specific databases and ontologies; task agents are designed to be efficient and effective tools.

Additionally, the goals of these respective systems are often presented as opposites: a lengthy conversation with a chitchat agent is generally perceived as successful, indicating user engagement and interest, whereas a prolonged conversation with a task-oriented agent is typically considered unsuccessful or suboptimal, suggesting that the user's needs were not met or were met with difficulty.

However, these distinctions are not as clear-cut when it comes to human communication. Most language is not purely transactional[1] or interactional[2] but a mix of both. In fact, exchanges are generally better described as *primarily* transactional or interactional (Brown and Yule, 1983). In the context of task-oriented dialogues, a system that lacks the ability to exhibit remorse when making errors, display empathy when a user's favorite restaurant is unavailable, or address additional context such as having dinner with one's boss vs. with a friend hampers human-system collaboration.

### 1.1 Towards a More Comprehensive User Understanding

Several studies aim to add chitchat into TODs, such as Accentor (Sun et al., 2021) and FusedChat (Young et al., 2022). However, these methods only add *general* chitchat and do not focus on any specific skill. Not all chitchat may be useful in TODs and a more focused approach should be considered.

**Emotional State** Understanding a user's task-oriented needs is undeniably crucial. Nevertheless, going beyond that and taking into account their emotional state can result in more suitable responses. It can also compensate for system errors, and even create the impression of a more capable system (Lutfi et al., 2013), ultimately leading to enhanced user satisfaction. Chitchat systems have greatly benefited from emotion detection, enabling them to generate more empathetic responses. I believe this skill can also enhance task-oriented systems, allowing them to better grasp the nuances of user utterances, resulting in more relevant and personalized responses.

To facilitate this, the EmoWOZ dataset (Feng et al., 2022) annotates user turns from the MultiWOZ corpus (Budzianowski et al., 2018) with emotion labels. In my research, I have explored an initial approach called JEmToD (Joint End-to-End Modeling of Emotion Detection and Task-Oriented Dialogue) which generates emotion labels, belief state, dialogue acts and system responses based on a given dialogue history. I have found that although this additional task does not hinder task-oriented performance, it does not improve empathy in system responses and does not provide enough grounding. To address this, I intend to investigate ways of more explicitly conditioning system responses on user emotions. For example, one approach could involve passing JEMTOD's output to a Large Language Model (LLM), instructing it to reformulate JEMTOD's response based on the predicted emotion label.

**Beyond the Database** A conversation is situated, meaning that contextual information may naturally be introduced. This act can be initiated by the system, to incorporate more diversity and make the dialogue more engaging. The KETOD dataset (Chen et al., 2022) focuses on this effort. System responses rely on relevant information retrieved from Wikipedia about proposed entities and annotators rewrite the original responses to integrate this new information. I plan to experiment with models

[1] the goal is external to the encounter and leads to performing an action, for example.

[2] the goal is internal to the encounter and pertains to the relationship between participants.



*Proceedings of the 19th Annual Meeting of the Young Reseachers' Roundtable on Spoken Dialogue Systems*, pages 30–32
September 11–12, 2023. 

trained on this dataset.

This act may also be initiated by users, as they naturally provide contextual details. Indeed, it is important to acknowledge that users often have multiple, possibly underlying, goals such as needing to blow off steam after a long day, impressing one's significant other, or simply avoiding boredom. This background information may surface during a task-oriented conversation, as elements of backstory or justification of the request are introduced. However, these details tend to either be treated as noise by most task-oriented systems or cause confusion and break down the dialogue. This is quite unlike chitchat systems, trained on dialogues grounded in personas, situations, and general knowledge. We aim to explore avenues for enhancing TOD datasets in a similar manner, leveraging LLMs to do so automatically, as far as possible.

## 2 Spoken dialogue system (SDS) research

Predicting the state of SDS in the next 5 or even 10 years is challenging due to the rapid evolution of the field. However, it is clear that SDS and text-based dialogue systems are here to stay, offering a convenient means of interacting with machines for non-specialist users, in turn generating increased interest from actors in industry. This enthusiasm drives the direction of SDS towards more reliable systems (particularly in executing tasks like booking tickets or restaurant reservations) capable of providing accurate, relevant and non-hallucinated information. Another promising trend is the growing emphasis on personalization and adaptation of these agents to individual users' preferences, needs, and communication styles.

Leveraging the capabilities of LLMs for SDS presents an exciting opportunity for young researchers in the coming years. Understanding where LLMs fit in relation to TODs is an important topic. It raises questions such as: Can these models be employed in an end-to-end manner? Should they be utilized more prominently in specific components such as natural language understanding or natural language generation? Can they generate training data for early-stage prototyping while awaiting the collection of real-world data? Given their ability to follow instructions and generate coherent text, can they serve as user simulators that account for character traits/personas as well as task-oriented goals ?

While LLMs showcase powerful language capabilities, ensuring they provide precise, factual, and reliable information within narrow domains, as found in TODs, poses a non-trivial challenge. In this regard, research focusing on implementing safeguard mechanisms and constraints for these models needs to be carried out, especially if they are to be employed at scale in sensitive environments.

## 3 Suggested topics for discussion

- Where do LLMs fit in the task-oriented dialogue pipeline? Is it advisable to use them compared to smaller fine-tuned models?
- How can we enhance the contextual awareness of SDS, in the broad sense of taking into account user persona, situational factors such as a user's mood, open-domain knowledge and commonsense (Bosselut et al., 2019)?
- Human evaluation is often challenging and costly to conduct, however its significance is vital in assessing a system's performance. How can we simplify this evaluation? Is it viable for example to establish a platform that facilitates the pooling of efforts, allowing researchers to conveniently upload their systems for evaluation by fellow experts? Could a standard framework be created ?

## References

Antoine Bosselut, Hannah Rashkin, Maarten Sap, Chaitanya Malaviya, Asli Celikyilmaz, and Yejin Choi. 2019. COMET: Commonsense transformers for automatic knowledge graph construction. In *Proceedings of the 57th Annual Meeting of the Association for Computational Linguistics*. Association for Computational Linguistics, Florence, Italy, pages 4762–4779. https://doi.org/10.18653/v1/P19-1470.

Gillian Brown and George Yule. 1983. *Teaching the spoken language*, volume 2. Cambridge university press.

Paweł Budzianowski, Tsung-Hsien Wen, Bo-Hsiang Tseng, Iñigo Casanueva, Stefan Ultes, Osman Ramadan, and Milica Gašić. 2018. MultiWOZ - a large-scale multi-domain Wizard-of-Oz dataset for task-oriented dialogue modelling. In *Proceedings of the 2018 Conference on Empirical Methods in Natural Language Processing*. Association for Computational Linguistics, Brussels, Belgium, pages 5016–5026. https://doi.org/10.18653/v1/D18-1547.

Zhiyu Chen, Bing Liu, Seungwhan Moon, Chinnadhurai Sankar, Paul Crook, and William Yang Wang. 2022. KETOD: Knowledge-enriched task-oriented dialogue. In *Findings of the Association for Computational Linguistics: NAACL 2022*. Association for Computational Linguistics, Seattle, United States, pages 2581–2593. https://doi.org/10.18653/v1/2022.findings-naacl.197.

Shutong Feng, Nurul Lubis, Christian Geishauser, Hsien-chin Lin, Michael Heck, Carel van Niekerk, and Milica Gasic. 2022. EmoWOZ: A large-scale corpus and labelling scheme for emotion recognition in task-oriented dialogue systems. In *Proceedings of the Thirteenth Language Resources and Evaluation Conference*. European Language Resources Association, Marseille, France, pages 4096–4113. https://aclanthology.org/2022.lrec-1.436.

Syaheerah Lutfi, Fernando Fernández-Martínez, Jaime Lorenzo-Trueba, Roberto Barra-Chicote, and Juan Montero. 2013. I feel you: The design and evaluation of a domotic affect-sensitive spoken conversational agent. *Sensors* 13(8):10519–10538. https://doi.org/10.3390/s130810519.

Kai Sun, Seungwhan Moon, Paul Crook, Stephen Roller, Becka Silvert, Bing Liu, Zhiguang Wang, Honglei Liu, Eunjoon Cho, and Claire Cardie. 2021. Adding chit-chat to enhance task-oriented dialogues. In *Proceedings of the 2021 Conference of the North American Chapter of the Association for Computational Linguistics: Human Language Technologies*. Association for Computational Linguistics, Online, pages 1570–1583. https://doi.org/10.18653/v1/2021.naacl-main.124.

Tom Young, Frank Xing, Vlad Pandelea, Jinjie Ni, and Erik Cambria. 2022. Fusing task-oriented and open-domain dialogues in conversational agents. In *Proceedings of the AAAI Conference on Artificial Intelligence*. volume 36, pages 11622–11629.

## Biographical sketch

Armand Stricker is a PhD student at Université Paris-Saclay in the LISN lab, working under the supervision of Patrick Paroubek. His research interests lie in task-oriented dialogues, open-domain dialogues, and in their interaction. Prior to his PhD, Armand completed a master's degree in English as well as a master's in Natural Language Processing at the Université de Paris. As part of his master's thesis, he worked on temporal question-answering. He enjoys swimming, biking, running and discovering new places.

# Livia Qian

KTH Royal Institute of Technology
Lindstedtsvägen 24, floor 5
Stockholm, Sweden
114 28

liviaq@kth.se


## 1 Research interests

My research interests lie generally in the area of **natural language processing (NLP)**, **text-to-speech (TTS)** and **automatic speech recognition (ASR)**, with a special focus on **dialogue modeling** with both **supervised** and **unsupervised learning**.

With respect to spoken dialogues, I focus on creating representations that can **model prosody**, turn shifts, pauses, backchannels and improve the accuracy of two-channel speech generation, as well as solve downstream tasks like emotion and laughter detection. I am also interested in **online ASR** and **speech synthesis** for dialogues.

With respect to written dialogues, I aim to improve spoken dialogue representations with text and other modalities through **multimodal learning**, as is common in ASR. I also try to improve language models using other modalities like speech, among others (e.g., vision and motion), and solve less-researched dialogue tasks using language models (like **reference resolution (RR)** and **coreference resolution (CRR)**).

### 1.1 Resolving References in Visually-Grounded Dialogue via Text Generation

RR is about finding linguistic elements that are semantically related or refer to the same entity. CRR is similar but instead of connecting textual elements, it resolves references to entities in other modalities. In our case, we tried to identify references to images in dialogues. This is challenging because information can be scattered across the dialogue history and pronouns are especially hard to resolve, e.g., when used by multiple speakers.

We used the dataset *A Game of Sorts* by Willemsen et al. (2022). It consists of dialogues in which pairs of speakers were tasked with ranking a set of images based on predefined criteria. The points at which the speakers referred to specific images were marked during data collection, thus making it possible to connect the mentions and utterances to the images.

The modeling consists of two steps: first, we fine-tuned a language model (GPT-2 and GPT-3) to summarize what the speakers said about the different images up to a certain point in a dialogue; in each case, the reference(s) in the most recent utterances are pointed out to indicate which image(s) we are interested in generating the summaries for, for which the model is supposed to use the previous mentions belonging to the very same image(s). After this, the caption-like summaries were passed to a vision-language model to identify the most likely images. The correctness of the generated summaries were compared against simple pronoun substitutions and the state-of-the-art models in CRR.

The paper (Willemsen et al., 2023) has been accepted at SIGDIAL 2023. We showed that discourse processing is possible to frame as a causal language learning problem and that large language models can be fine-tuned to generate referent descriptions.

### 1.2 ASR on multi-channel dialogues

The field of ASR is widely addressed by the research community, but does not work well on dialogues where there is overlapping speech or different adversarial effects (e.g., backchannels). I am working on two-speaker ASR by conditioning the speech representations of the two channels on each other before connecting them with their respective transcripts. There is a possibility for extending this to on-the-fly (online) speech recognition.

The resulting models and representations could be used to solve different downstream tasks, e.g., turn taking and emotion detection, as well as speech synthesis and NLP-related tasks. Such models could improve the conversational skills of social robots or the time-alignment of video transcripts. These tasks have not received not much attention in text-based large language models (LLMs) as the main focus has been laid on content and memory improvement, but with the emergence of multimodal NLP and LLM-based chatbots, aspects like turn taking could be crucial to improve the flow of the conversation.

### 1.3 Dialogue speech synthesis

I might also consider working on speech synthesis. Some issues within this field are that there is usually not enough data to train on and that the generated speech is not expressive enough. Although current systems are enough for many use-cases, there is room for improvement in many aspects, e.g., delivery, prosody expression, controllable pauses and long-term effects. I think that speech synthesis may benefit from the speech representations from my other projects, especially in relation to dialogues where these aspects are highly dependent on context.



*Proceedings of the 19th Annual Meeting of the Young Reseachers' Roundtable on Spoken Dialogue Systems*, pages 33–34
September 11–12, 2023. 

## 2 Spoken dialogue system (SDS) research

**Where do you think the field of dialogue research will be in 5 to 10 years?** Dialogue research is becoming more and more important as TTS, speech-to-text (STT) and language models work fairly well on monologues, continuous text and short snippets (e.g., sentences) but do not usually take into account data more complex that these. Dialogues can also provide context that is often missing from monologues (e.g., disambiguation of terms and affirmation) which can aid in better response generation when it comes to speech synthesis, for example. What I think will improve in the upcoming years is the connection between content and prosody as well as other non-verbal cues.

**What do you think this generation of young researchers could accomplish in that time?** Young researchers can improve the fine-grained details to make conversations more human-like, with respect to both content and the naturalness of non-verbal signs. Another thing that is worth looking into is how to make use of long-term dependencies (similarly to how language models do) and representing dialogue history (previous dialogue sessions) by compressing previous information.

**What kind of questions need to be investigated to get the field to that point?** I think it is really important to create high-quality representations similar to wav2vec and HuBERT but for dialogues and dialogue context, either with the inclusion of prosody or separately from it.

**What are the most important things for users of SDSs?** Natural-sounding speech, informativeness and correctness of generated responses, identifying turn shifts in online systems, knowledge and visual grounding, correct reaction to human emotions, multimodal cues.

**Is there a difference between SDS research in academia and industry?** Industry and commissioned research are more profit-oriented than general academic research, and as such, they focus on hands-on and immediate applications. This narrows down the possible research questions, creates the need for patents and NDAs and requires system integration (e.g., in video games).

**Will SDSs be more widely used in the future? How? In what scenarios?** As TTS and ASR are considered to be solved for many use-cases, the areas where SDS can be used becomes more and more niche. Nevertheless, as mentioned before, the dialogue system of robots could greatly benefit from this field, as well as interactive GPS systems, general-use chatbots, personal assistants, video game scripts and video transcriptions (especially for interviews and movie subtitles).

## 3 Suggested topics for discussion

- How to keep up with the rapid development of large language models? How can SDS benefit from this? How can we improve models to keep up the pace?
- Can SDS research focus on paralinguistic elements while making use of the recent advancements in NLP to focus on the purely linguistic aspects? What kind of linguistic concepts could be useful to address and apply?
- Multi-model learning: how can SDS be combined with other modalities (e.g., vision, text, gestures)? What is the state-of-the-art in these topics?
- Modular vs. holistic models.
- Augmenting spoken dialogue data: how could we address the lack of data as a common problem in this field? What about speaker variation and prosody?
- Standardized frameworks and libraries. Common ways to do ablation studies.
- Frameworks and repositories for setting up user studies and data collection. Useful datasets.

## References


Bram Willemsen, Dmytro Kalpakchi, and Gabriel Skantze. 2022. Collecting Visually-Grounded Dialogue with A Game Of Sorts. In *Proceedings of the Thirteenth Language Resources and Evaluation Conference*. European Language Resources Association, Marseille, France, pages 2257–2268. https://aclanthology.org/2022.lrec-1.242.

Bram Willemsen, Livia Qian, and Gabriel Skantze. 2023. Resolving References in Visually-Grounded Dialogue via Text Generation (under review). In *SIGdial, ACL Anthology*.


## Biographical sketch

Livia Qian is a PhD student at KTH Royal Institute of Technology in Stockholm, Sweden. Her research interests include NLP, ASR and representation learning. Her PhD project is about representing spoken and written dialogues using machine learning models. Her current work focuses on multi-channel ASR for improving turn-shift detection and backchannel transcription, among others.

Livia has a Bachelor's degree in Computer Science a Master's degree in Machine Learning. Before joining academia, she worked at an IT company as a software developer. Her extra-curricular interests include board games, language learning and swimming.

**Iwona Christop**

Adam Mickiewicz University
Wieniawskiego 1
61-712 Poznań
iwochr2@st.amu.edu.pl

# 1 Research interests

## 1.1 Deep learning in audio classification

My main area of research interest is the use of **deep learning** methods in the classification of audio recordings, with a particular focus on **emotion recognition in speech** and **deep fake detection**.

**Speech emotion recognition** is an interdisciplinary problem combining psychology, physics, and computer science. By incorporating deep learning techniques, we can enhance spoken dialogue systems and improve their ability to understand users' emotional states. This solution has many applications, including adaptable interfaces, speech analysis for research purposes, and healthcare applications, where it could provide insight into patients' well-being.

As part of my Master's thesis, I am using pre-trained neural models such as Whisper by OpenAI (Radford et al. (2022)) and Wav2Vec2 by Facebook AI (Baevski et al. (2020)) to develop a robust system that can classify emotions in speech. As there is a visible lack of resources in this area, I am also creating a dataset of emotionally charged speech in Polish. By doing so, I hope to contribute to the advancement of research in the future.

As mentioned, my research interests also include the detection of deep fake audio. **Voice conversion techniques** are developing rapidly, and nowadays, one can easily preserve linguistic and semantic information of an utterance while manipulating the speaker's identity, prosody, and emotions. While these techniques have enormous potential, they also raise concerns. As such recordings are difficult to distinguish from real ones, it becomes harder to protect people against the spread of fake news, identity theft, and reputational damage (Kawa et al. (2022)).

I believe that developing models that use **deep learning techniques** to classify audio recordings is particularly important today. It is incredibly easy to come across fake news, which can greatly affect the society.

## 1.2 Sign languages

My second area of interest is **sign language**, which is often forgotten in the context of **dialogue systems**.

The world familiar to most people is unsuitable for deaf people, mainly due to communication barriers. For this reason, taking measures to guarantee better access to goods and services is crucial to enable deaf people to participate in social and public life.

A significant problem, which most people are not aware of, is that there is a large group of deaf people who cannot read or write in the native languages such as English or Polish.

In many institutions, deaf people cannot use an interpreter, making contact with a doctor, teacher, or police officer often impossible. The personnel of institutions is not familiar with the needs and problems of the Deaf, so they often demand written communication or expect lip reading.

While researchers around the world pay attention to this group of languages, we must remember that each nationality not only has its own **sign language**, but also dialects. Thus, it is important that **Polish Sign Language** also receive attention.

In addition, **sign languages** are considered **low-resource languages** – currently there is not enough annotated data to do more extensive research.

The development of a **real-time translation** system would provide a significant change in accessibility for the Deaf. I think it's worth paying attention to **low-resource languages** and making **dialogue systems** available to everyone.

## 1.3 Multimodality in dialogue systems

During my master's studies, I had the opportunity to participate in a research and development project that resulted in creating AMUseBot, a **task-oriented dialogue system** designed to assist the user in completing multi-step tasks.

The main goal of the project was to create a system that will provide engaging experience and keep the user focused throughout the conversation. In order to meet these objectives, we introduced two novel approaches – **dynamic multimodal communication** and **graph-based task management**.

The system's architecture follows standard baseline and it includes several modules responsible for specific **natural language processing** tasks – **automatic speech recognition**, **natural language understanding**, **dialogue management**, **natural language generation**, and **text-to-speech**.

As mentioned, the primary novelty is **graph-based**



*Proceedings of the 19th Annual Meeting of the Young Reseachers' Roundtable on Spoken Dialogue Systems*, pages 35–36
September 11–12, 2023. ©2023 Association for Computational Linguistics

**task management**. It effectively organizes the flow of dialogue and provides the user with visual cues during the conversation. A graph consists of a conversation history, with edges containing the user's statements and vertices containing the system's responses. With this representation, the visualization significantly improves user experience.

In addition, to ensure an engaging conversation, we gave the system different personalities. In the basic version, the user can choose from three options – default short commands, a kind chef who pays attention to details, and Gordon Ramsay.

Tests with users showed that the **multimodal approach** significantly increased their engagement and made the conversation more realistic.

The system was awarded an honorable mention in the research and development project competition at the AI Tech Summer School. The process of developing the system was described in the article "AMUseBot: Towards making the most out of a task-oriented dialogue system", published in the monograph "Progress in Polish Artificial Intelligence Research 4" (Christop et al. (2023)).

## 2 Spoken dialogue system (SDS) research

Currently, the biggest issue with **dialogue systems** is hallucination – they generate grammatically correct texts that are contentually incorrect. Research should therefore focus on creating chatbots that are able to back up their statements with relevant sources. To achieve this, young researchers should focus first and foremost on developing good quality data and extracting valuable information. This is the basis for obtaining substantively correct and satisfactory results.

The accuracy of information is also important for users. They should be able to get reliable answers with prompts that do not require specialized knowledge. In addition, **multimodality**, such as 3D models or human-like robots, should be used to provide a more realistic experience.

Nowadays, academic research is more focused on low-resource issues. These are matters that require attention but do not generate income. Companies, on the other hand, prefer to focus on more profitable ventures. Finding balance between both approaches is crucial to the development of **dialogue systems**.

It is worth pursuing research on **dialogue systems**, as they will be used even more extensively in the future – especially in the form of virtual assistants, helpline assistance, or emergency calls.

## 3 Suggested topics for discussion

- Using anthropomorphism to improve human-machine interaction – is speech emotion recognition too much?
- The gap between spoken and sign language: data acquisition methods and technological solutions.
- Leveraging multimodality in times of narrowing attention span.

## References

Alexei Baevski, Henry Zhou, Abdelrahman Mohamed, and Michael Auli. 2020. Wav2vec 2.0: A framework for self-supervised learning of speech representations. Curran Associates Inc., Red Hook, NY, USA, NIPS'20.

Iwona Christop, Kacper Dudzic, and Mikołaj Krzymiński. 2023. Amusebot: Towards making the most out of a task-oriented dialogue system. *Progress in Polish Artificial Intelligence Research 4* .

Piotr Kawa, Marcin Plata, and Piotr Syga. 2022. Specrnet: Towards faster and more accessible audio deepfake detection.

Alec Radford, Jong Wook Kim, Tao Xu, Greg Brockman, Christine McLeavey, and Ilya Sutskever. 2022. Robust speech recognition via large-scale weak supervision .

## Biographical sketch

Iwona Christop is a MSc student in the field of Artificial Intelligence. Her Master thesis topic is "Speech Emotion Recognition using pre-trained neural models". She is a holder of a BSc in Computer Science, and completed courses in Acoustics and Polish Sign Language.

She is a co-author of an article published in the monograph "Progress in Polish Artificial Intelligence Research 4" and has had the opportunity to present her work at conferences such as Polish Conference on Artificial Intelligence 2023 and the US-Poland Science and Technology Symposium 2023 in Silicon Valley. In addition, she has been a participant in such events as Data Science Summit 2022, the 17th Conference of the European Chapter of the Association for Computational Linguistics, and the 24th Annual Conference of The European Association for Machine Translation.

# Lucas Druart

Orange
2 Avevnue de Belle Fontaine
35510 Cesson-Sévigné
France

lucas1.druart@orange.com
lucas.druart@alumni.univ-avignon.fr
https://lucasdruart.github.io/


## 1 Research interests

Task-Oriented Dialogue (TOD) systems provide interactive assistance to a user in order to accomplish a specific task such as making a reservation at a restaurant or booking a room in a hotel.

Speech presents itself as a natural interface for TOD systems. A typical approach to implement them is to use a modular architecture (Gao et al., 2018). A core component of such dialogue systems is Spoken Language Understanding (SLU) whose goal is to extract the relevant information from the user's utterances. While spoken dialogue was the focus of earlier work (Williams et al., 2013; Henderson et al., 2014), recent work has focused on text inputs with no regard for the specificities of spoken language (Wu et al., 2019; Heck et al., 2020; Feng et al., 2021). However, this approach fails to account for the differences between written and spoken language (Faruqui and Hakkani-Tür, 2022) such as disfluencies.

My research focuses on **Spoken Language Understanding** in the context of **Task-Oriented Dialogue**. More specifically I am interested in the two following research directions:

- **Annotation** schema for **spoken** TODs,
- Propagation of **dialogue history** for **contextually coherent** predictions.

### 1.1 Annotation schema for spoken TODs

Chat TODs corpora benefit from a wide diversity of semantic annotation schema which have different levels of precision. The Slot-Value scheme is probably the most commonly used one, such as for the Dialogue State Tracking (DST) annotations of Multi-Woz (Budzianowski et al., 2018). However this scheme lacks grounding (*e.g.* two mentions of the same entity are seen as two separate values) which is a fundamental aspect of human-human interactions (Benotti and Blackburn, 2021). It also does not provide dynamic links between the mentioned entities[1] which can be essential to co-reference resolution. For instance, when a user booking a hotel room refers to the previously mentioned hotel by its address such as "I would like to book the one in Prague.", the link between a hotel and its address becomes essential.

More recent schema such as Dialogue-AMR (Bonial et al., 2020) and Dialogue Meaning Representation (DMR) (Hu et al., 2022) address these shortcomings by relying on the same mechanisms as Abstract Meaning Representation (AMR) (Banarescu et al., 2013). Users of spoken dialogue system (SDS) tend to refer to previously mentioned entities by their characteristics which change over the course of the dialogue. The hierarchical relations defined in DMR track those relations thus enabling direct disambiguation. Dialogue-AMR further maps it to specific robotic controls.

I believe such rich annotation scheme will help address spoken TODs specificities and I am currently working on such a scheme for the MEDIA spoken TOD dataset (Devillers et al., 2004).

### 1.2 Dialogue history propagation

For TOD systems to help users accomplish complex tasks, such as choosing the most relevant hotel to a user requirements, it must take into account the information provided in previous turns. Dialogue history is thus crucial information for contextually accurate and consistent predictions. However it remains unclear how to propagate such context in a spoken dialogue understanding model's predictions.

During the recent Speech Aware Dialogue Systems Technology Challenge (Soltau et al., 2022) all proposed systems aggregated the dialogue history once transcribed, including our system (Jacqmin et al., 2023) which ranked first. End-to-End models, which benefit from joint-optimization, require more sophisticated mechanism to limit the input size.

[1]Note that definition of slot types often imply some static relations between the slots. For instance in Multi-Woz DST annotations slots are grouped by domain.



*Proceedings of the 19th Annual Meeting of the Young Reseachers' Roundtable on Spoken Dialogue Systems*, pages 37–39
September 11–12, 2023. 

I am currently exploring different fusion strategies between a textual semantic context and audio extracted features (*e.g.* two cross attention modules each attending to an encoder, modality fusion before the decoder).

## 2 SDS research

The Spoken Dialogue System field is moving at an incredibly fast pace and the gap between research and deployment is narrowing. Therefore I believe future research will have to rely on more realistic datasets.

- Such datasets should provide a database of entities given that all errors do not lead to a wrong entity matching.
- The very interactive nature of SDS implies that a misunderstanding at a given turn can change how the next turns unfold. I believe future datasets should be dynamic and provide several continuations at each turn. This will enable researchers to measure which misunderstandings lead to poorer dialogue trajectories.
- Some chat corpora have been vocalized to benefit from the large quantity of data of such corpora. However SDS research also requires natural speech datasets to take into account the specific interactions (*e.g.* confirmations, repetitions, turn taking) of spoken dialogues.

Finally evaluating the impact of SDS components on the completion of the targeted task seems to be a promising and mandatory research path.

## 3 Suggested topics for discussion

In a broader discussion I believe the following topics might be interesting to discuss:

- While generative models are displaying impressive capacities they may not provide a reliable and consistent behavior. For instance when SDS are connected to APIs, it becomes essential to include some control over the inputs of the APIs. Hence I believe discussing techniques to secure the use of such models in SDS might prove helpful.
- Prompting techniques are being widely adopted, however we have only little understanding of how they work. I believe sharing our experience and knowledge of prompting can provide indications of what seems to happen internally with prompts. For instance, one might wonder if any type of information (*e.g.* structured, audio, image) can be passed as a prompt.
- Finally I believe SDS research should take into account its ethical implications such as the greenhouse gas emission burden of deep learning or the anthropomorphic relation users tend to develop with dialogue systems. Investigating computing wise efficiency and human computer interaction in the context of SDS might help move forward in both directions.

## References


Laura Banarescu, Claire Bonial, Shu Cai, Madalina Georgescu, Kira Griffitt, Ulf Hermjakob, Kevin Knight, Philipp Koehn, Martha Palmer, and Nathan Schneider. 2013. Abstract Meaning Representation for sembanking. In *Proceedings of the 7th Linguistic Annotation Workshop and Interoperability with Discourse*. Association for Computational Linguistics, Sofia, Bulgaria, pages 178–186. https://aclanthology.org/W13-2322.

Luciana Benotti and Patrick Blackburn. 2021. Grounding as a collaborative process. In *Proceedings of the 16th Conference of the European Chapter of the Association for Computational Linguistics: Main Volume*. Association for Computational Linguistics, Online, pages 515–531. https://doi.org/10.18653/v1/2021.eacl-main.41.

Claire Bonial, Lucia Donatelli, Mitchell Abrams, Stephanie M. Lukin, Stephen Tratz, Matthew Marge, Ron Artstein, David Traum, and Clare Voss. 2020. Dialogue-AMR: Abstract Meaning Representation for dialogue. In *Proceedings of the Twelfth Language Resources and Evaluation Conference*. European Language Resources Association, Marseille, France, pages 684–695. https://aclanthology.org/2020.lrec-1.86.

Pawe\l Budzianowski, Tsung-Hsien Wen, Bo-Hsiang Tseng, Iñigo Casanueva, Stefan Ultes, Osman Ramadan, and Milica Gašić. 2018. MultiWOZ - A Large-Scale Multi-Domain Wizard-of-Oz Dataset for Task-Oriented Dialogue Modelling. In *Proceedings of the 2018 Conference on Empirical Methods in Natural Language Processing*. Association for Computational Linguistics, Brussels, Belgium, pages 5016–5026. https://doi.org/10.18653/v1/D18-1547.

Laurence Devillers, Hélène Bonneau-Maynard, Sophie Rosset, Patrick Paroubek, Kevin McTait, Djamel Mostefa, Khalid Choukri, Laurent Charnay, Caroline Bousquet-Vernhettes, Nadine Vigouroux, Frédéric Béchet, Laurent Romary, Jean-Yves Antoine, Jeanne Villaneau, Myriam Vergnes, and Jérôme Goulian. 2004. The french media/evalda project: the evaluation of the understanding capability of spoken language dialogue systems. In *International Conference on Language Resources and Evaluation*.

Manaal Faruqui and Dilek Hakkani-Tür. 2022. Revisiting the boundary between ASR and NLU in the age of conversational dialog systems. *Computational Linguistics* 48(1):221–232. https://doi.org/10.1162/coli_a_00430.

Yue Feng, Yang Wang, and Hang Li. 2021. A Sequence-to-Sequence Approach to Dialogue State Tracking. In *Proceedings of the 59th Annual Meeting of the Association for Computational Linguistics and the 11th International Joint Conference on Natural Language Processing (Volume 1: Long Papers)*. Association for Computational Linguistics, Online, pages 1714–1725. https://doi.org/10.18653/v1/2021.acl-long.135.

Jianfeng Gao, Michel Galley, and Lihong Li. 2018. Neural Approaches to Conversational AI. In *The 41st International ACM SIGIR Conference on Research & Development in Information Retrieval*. Association for Computing Machinery, New York, NY, USA, SIGIR '18, pages 1371–1374. https://doi.org/10.1145/3209978.3210183.

Michael Heck, Carel van Niekerk, Nurul Lubis, Christian Geishauser, Hsien-Chin Lin, Marco Moresi, and Milica Gasic. 2020. TripPy: A Triple Copy Strategy for Value Independent Neural Dialog State Tracking. In *Proceedings of the 21th Annual Meeting of the Special Interest Group on Discourse and Dialogue (SIGDIAL)*. Association for Computational Linguistics, 1st virtual meeting, pages 35–44. https://aclanthology.org/2020.sigdial-1.4.

Matthew Henderson, Blaise Thomson, and Jason D. Williams. 2014. The second dialog state tracking challenge. In *Proceedings of the 15th Annual Meeting of the Special Interest Group on Discourse and Dialogue (SIGDIAL)*. Association for Computational Linguistics, Philadelphia, PA, U.S.A., pages 263–272. https://doi.org/10.3115/v1/W14-4337.

Xiangkun Hu, Junqi Dai, Hang Yan, Yi Zhang, Qipeng Guo, Xipeng Qiu, and Zheng Zhang. 2022. Dialogue meaning representation for task-oriented dialogue systems. In *Findings of the Association for Computational Linguistics: EMNLP 2022*. Association for Computational Linguistics, Abu Dhabi, United Arab Emirates, pages 223–237. https://aclanthology.org/2022.findings-emnlp.17.

Léo Jacqmin, Lucas Druart, Valentin Vielzeuf, Lina Maria Rojas-Barahona, Yannick Estève, and Benoît Favre. 2023. Olisia: a cascade system for spoken dialogue state tracking.

Hagen Soltau, Izhak Shafran, Mingqiu Wang, Abhinav Rastogi, Jeffrey Zhao, Ye Jia, Wei Han, Yuan Cao, and Aramys Miranda. 2022. Speech aware dialog system technology challenge (dstc11).

Jason Williams, Antoine Raux, Deepak Ramachandran, and Alan Black. 2013. The Dialog State Tracking Challenge. In *Proceedings of the SIGDIAL 2013 Conference*. Association for Computational Linguistics, Metz, France, pages 404–413. https://aclanthology.org/W13-4065.

Chien-Sheng Wu, Andrea Madotto, Ehsan Hosseini-Asl, Caiming Xiong, Richard Socher, and Pascale Fung. 2019. Transferable Multi-Domain State Generator for Task-Oriented Dialogue Systems. In *Proceedings of the 57th Annual Meeting of the Association for Computational Linguistics*. Association for Computational Linguistics, Florence, Italy, pages 808–819. https://doi.org/10.18653/v1/P19-1078.

## Biographical sketch

Lucas Druart is a PhD student working jointly with Orange Labs and the Speech and Language Team of the University of Avignon. Previously he graduated from a double degree in applied mathematics and computer science, with a focus on Statistics and Machine Learning, from Grenoble-INP Ensimag and University of Grenoble Alpes (UGA). His current research interests include Natural Language Processing, Spoken Language Understanding and Task-Oriented Dialogue.

Kacper Dudzic

Adam Mickiewicz University
Wieniawskiego 1
61-712 Poznań
Poland
kacdud1@amu.edu.pl

## 1 Research interests

My research interests can be broadly categorized into the areas of **natural language understanding** and **multi-modal dialogue systems**.

### 1.1 Global context for natural language understanding

My main topic of interest is **global context for natural language understanding**. As a shallow analogy to human conversation, the understanding of the user's utterances by a dialogue system can be improved by supplying it with additional context constituting the greater „whole" of the conversation, such as dialogue history.

In my ongoing master's thesis, I describe various sources of global context and analyze the effect appending some of their configurations to user utterances has on a natural language understanding module's performance. I consider intra-systemic sources where the extra information is already present in the system, for example, dialogue history or previously identified dialogue acts and slot values, and – inspired by such approaches as Xu et al. (2021) – extra-systemic ones, where the information is taken from the outside, e.g., WordNet definitions of words present in a given utterance. As the main part of the thesis, I conduct a series of experiments with the use of a T5-based natural language understanding module and the MultiWOZ dataset. By comparing the performance of several versions of the module fine-tuned with samples enriched with global context in various ways against a baseline, I show that overall the use of global context translates into better performance of the module.

### 1.2 Multi-modal dialogue systems

Conversations with dialogue systems are often not easy for the users: as various evaluation studies show (Adamopoulou and Moussiades, 2020), they tend to give up mid-conversation, get frustrated easily, or end up rating the whole ordeal poorly. My second topic of interest is the theory and practice relating to **multi-modal dialogue systems**, which are one of the potential solutions to such problems. By engaging the user through multiple modalities, it is easier to draw his attention and keep him focused on the task at hand, allowing the conversation to continue in cases where it might have ended prematurely.

Recently, along with a team of other students from my university, I finished the development of AMUseBot, a task-oriented dialogue system envisioned as a cooking assistant, previously presented at the 4th Polish Conference on Artificial Intelligence in Łódź in the form of a poster and a publication (Christop et al., 2023) describing the work-in-progress stage of the project. AMUseBot communicates with users simultaneously through text, voice, and a graphical display, putting the principles of multi-modal communication into practice. It also employs a mix of rule-based and machine learning-based modules, enabling a controlled „main scenario" dialogue progress while simultaneously being able to understand and reply to more open-ended user utterances in a robust manner.

## 2 Spoken dialogue system (SDS) research

- **Where do you think the field of dialogue research will be in 5 to 10 years?** I think that the field of dialogue research is bound to rise in importance by a large margin. Besides personal assistants becoming vastly more capable and, ergo, more ubiquitous over the next few years, I suspect that a relatively new avenue for dialogue system research will open up – embedded SDSs. By that, I mean systems integrated with websites, electronic appliances, buildings, etc., acting as an interface layer of sorts, enabling querying dedicated databases containing information about a company, product, and the like, in natural language.

- **What do you think this generation of young researchers could accomplish in that time?** I think it will be a perfect time to be a young researcher. Even now, there is a vast array of opportunities relating to both implementing recent research findings in practice and also pushing the theoretical side of the field forward. The current climate of natural language processing research might be a bubble, at least to some extent, but it need not devalue the accomplishments of the researchers in the near future. It is a unique opportunity that should not be missed.



*Proceedings of the 19th Annual Meeting of the Young Reseachers' Roundtable on Spoken Dialogue Systems*, pages 40–41
September 11–12, 2023. 

- **What kind of questions need to be investigated to get the field to that point?** I believe that the field can go far just with the current momentum. Nevertheless, I would like to see more attention being brought to ethical and social issues of SDSs deployment so that the field does not only go forward but also in the right direction. As the capabilities of such systems increase, so too do their influence on society and the responsibility of their creators.

- **What are the most important things for users of SDSs** In my opinion, one of the most important things for users of SDSs is the feeling that the system inhabits the same world as they do. I feel like there is still work to be done in regard to creating robust systems that not only talk in a natural, engaging way but also do not include false, nonsensical, or ambiguous information „not from this world" in their utterances without resorting to rule-based architectures.

- **Is there a difference between SDS research in academia and industry?** In the broader context of natural language processing research, currently, a growing divide between academia and industry can be observed in terms of available resources, with the industry leaving academia behind. Considering the current paradigm revolving around large language models, some predict academia to become relegated to a „secondary" role, being limited to, e.g., evaluation of models developed by private companies. I am very interested in alternative, more optimistic perspectives regarding this issue or ideas relating to preventing the pessimistic one.

- **Will SDSs be more widely used in the future? How? In what scenarios?** With the somewhat recent advances (and, more importantly, public recognition) of generative AI, I think that in the future, SDSs will be used way more widely, albeit we can expect to mainly see more conversational systems focused only on holding a natural-sounding conversation with a user without a task component involved. Nevertheless, I think that in the long run, this will also bring attention to research aimed at supplementing task-oriented SDSs with controlled (grounded) generative modules.

## 3 Suggested topics for discussion

- The importance of additional sources of knowledge in SDSs: global context, ontologies, external knowledge bases, grounding, etc. Are such solutions necessary in the long run? Or is further pure compute scaling sustainable?

- Is developing a robust test for measuring high-level natural language understanding that will not fall prey to the AI effect like the Turing test possible? What could it look like?

- Long-term perspectives for transformer-based models in the dialogue domain. Can we expect future breakthroughs without changing the current paradigm?

- Is there potential in integrating SDSs with embodied AI agents? What are the implications of such a synthesis?

## References


Eleni Adamopoulou and Lefteris Moussiades. 2020. Chatbots: History, technology, and applications. *Machine Learning with Applications* 2:100006. https://doi.org/10.1016/j.mlwa.2020.100006.

Iwona Christop, Kacper Dudzic, and Mikołaj Krzymiński. 2023. Amusebot: Towards making the most out of a task-oriented dialogue system. *Progress in Polish Artificial Intelligence Research* 4, forthcoming.

Ruochen Xu, Yuwei Fang, Chenguang Zhu, and Michael Zeng. 2021. Does knowledge help general nlu? an empirical study. *CoRR* abs/2109.00563. https://arxiv.org/abs/2109.00563.


## Biographical sketch

Kacper Dudzic is a student at the Adam Mickiewicz University in Poznań (Poland), in his last year of a master's degree in Artificial Intelligence. As a part of his master's thesis, he is investigating the role of global context for user utterance disambiguation in dialogue systems. He also holds a master's degree in Japanese Linguistics from the same university with a diploma thesis focused on linguistic issues of Japanese-Polish machine translation. His academic interests include natural language understanding in the context of dialogue systems, large language model research, and various other topics at the intersection of computer science and linguistics. Currently, he is employed at the Center for Artificial Intelligence at his home university. Before that, he worked as a language modeling engineer at VoiceLab.AI[1], the creator of the first Polish ChatGPT-like AI assistant, TRURL. He wants to start a Ph.D. in natural language processing next year.

[1] https://voicelab.ai/

# Selina Meyer

Regensburg University
Germany

selina.meyer@ur.de
https://selinameyer.github.io


## 1 Research interests

My PhD focuses on conversational agents for behaviour change, with a focus on the feasibility of applying Large Language Models (LLMs) such as GPT-4 in this context.

### 1.1 Prompt Engineering and Conversational Framework Design for LLMs for Wellbeing

I designed a conversational framework based on Motivational Interviewing theory, a client-centered therapy approach that emphasizes open questions and reflections to help clients find their own reasons and strategies for change Miller and Rollnick (2002); Clifford and Curtis (2016). The framework classifies user turns with codes relevant for behaviour change Miller et al. (2003) and selects a counsellor behaviour to be prompted to GPT-4 based on the user utterance type. I will evaluate to what extent GPT can be controlled in this context using the prompt engineering techniques employed in the conversational framework, and what current restraints of such models are in the context of interactions that rely on deeply social behaviours such as empathy and conveying an understanding of underlying expressed emotions and thoughts. In this context, I am also exploring how to mitigate potential harms of using such a technology in the context of behaviour change. To achieve this, it is important to define how LLM-output in the context of empathy and therapist-client interactions can be evaluated. Thus, I am interested in evaluation metrics for NLG in niche contexts where no ground truth is available, such as Sharma et al. (2020); Welivita and Pu (2020). In the same vein, I want to explore methods of harm mitigation, for instance caused by unhelpful advice or reinforcing negative behaviours if misused (i.e. supporting weight loss for anorexic users).

### 1.2 Effects of LLM-driven Motivational Chatbot on Behaviour Change Motivation

For the remainder of my PhD, I will mainly focus on the effects a conversational agent using the created conversational framework has on motivation and readiness to change behaviour. To do this, I will run two user studies, the first utilizing situated work task situations, where participants are requested to imagine they want to pursue a specific behaviour change before conversing with the chatbot. In this user study, we will measure whether the framework created leads to higher therapeutic alignment, user engagement, and perceived empathy and competence than a LLM-based chatbot that does not use the framework. The measures we will employ are based on similar research by He et al. (2022). The text data collected in this study will be analysed with regard to the quality of conversation and potentially harmful LLM-outputs. I will also explore, to what extent user behaviour influences the quality of the conversation. For instance, I hypothesize, that conversations with shorter user utterances might be less successful, as they give the chatbot less to work with.

In the second study, we will then test the conversational agent on people who are actually interested in changing their own behaviour. In this study, we will also measure effects of the chatbot on self-efficacy, readiness to change, and goal reflection. Participants will fill out all three measures both before and after the interaction with the chatbot. An increase in readiness to change, self-efficacy, or goal reflection will be a sign of the success of the intervention and the feasibility of using the chatbot to increase motivation for behaviour change. In future work, these evaluations could be complemented by a longer term study which investigates effects on behaviour change success.

## 2 Spoken dialogue system (SDS) research

I believe, that ChatGPT has caused a paradigm shift in the field of conversational AI research. Not only has it led to new opportunities of research, it also put chatbots on the map for the general population. This leads to a wider understanding of conversational AI and SDS in the general population. However, this also has the potential of leading to the privatization of conversational AI and SDS research, as it becomes harder and harder for researchers to compete with the financial prerequisites and manpower in industry. On the other hand, it could also mean increased collaboration between industry and academic research.

Ethical design is also a challenge that becomes increasingly important in times of LLMs. The curation of less biased datasets for training, the mitigation of the environmental impact of LLMs, and the containment of low-paid, unethical labour employed by industry creators of such models all call for solutions, which leave a rich gap for ethical research in the context of large models for con-



*Proceedings of the 19th Annual Meeting of the Young Reseachers' Roundtable on Spoken Dialogue Systems*, pages 42–43
September 11–12, 2023. ©2023 Association for Computational Linguistics

versational AI.

## 3 Suggested topics for discussion

Here, authors will suggest three topics for discussion in the discussion panels during the event. As an example, here are some of the discussion topics discussed in previous workshops:

- Evaluation of LLM-outputs when no ground truth/gold data is available
- Controllability of LLM-based text generation
- How can researchers compete with industry considering the difference in funding and manpower?

It is recommended to suggest topics, on which the author has knowledge, but also topics that they find interesting and relevant to the young community.

## References


Dawn Clifford and Laura Curtis. 2016. *Motivational interviewing in nutrition and fitness*. Guilford Publications.

Linwei He, Erkan Basar, Reinout W Wiers, Marjolijn L Antheunis, and Emiel Krahmer. 2022. Can chatbots help to motivate smoking cessation? a study on the effectiveness of motivational interviewing on engagement and therapeutic alliance. *BMC Public Health* 22(1):726.

William R Miller, Theresa B Moyers, Denise Ernst, and Paul Amrhein. 2003. Manual for the motivational interviewing skill code (misc). *Unpublished manuscript. Albuquerque: Center on Alcoholism, Substance Abuse and Addictions, University of New Mexico* .

William R Miller and Stephen Rollnick. 2002. *Motivational Interviewing, Second Edition: Preparing People for Change*. Applications of Motivational Interviewing Series. Guilford Publications.

Ashish Sharma, Adam Miner, David Atkins, and Tim Althoff. 2020. A computational approach to understanding empathy expressed in text-based mental health support. In *Proceedings of the 2020 Conference on Empirical Methods in Natural Language Processing (EMNLP)*. Association for Computational Linguistics, Online, pages 5263–5276. https://doi.org/10.18653/v1/2020.emnlp-main.425.

Anuradha Welivita and Pearl Pu. 2020. A taxonomy of empathetic response intents in human social conversations. In *Proceedings of the 28th International Conference on Computational Linguistics*. International Committee on Computational Linguistics, Barcelona, Spain (Online), pages 4886–4899. https://doi.org/10.18653/v1/2020.coling-main.429.


## Biographical sketch

Selina Meyer is a third-year PhD student and research assistant at the Chair for Information Science of Regensburg University, Germany. With a background in the humanities, she is primarily interested in behavioural and user-centered aspects of computer science and its application in social sciences.

**Sourabrata Mukherjee**

Charles University, Faculty of Mathematics and Physics
Institute of Formal and Applied Linguistics
Prague, Czech Republic
mukherjee@ufal.mff.cuni.cz

## 1 Research interests

My primary research focus lies in the domain of *Text Style Transfer (TST)*, a fascinating area within Natural Language Processing (NLP). *TST* involves the transformation of text into a desired style while approximately preserving its underlying content. In my research, I am also driven by the goal of incorporating *TST* techniques into NLP systems, particularly within the realm of dialogue systems. I am intrigued by the concept of *Stylized Dialog Response Generation*, which aims to enhance the versatility and adaptability of dialog systems in generating text responses with specific style attributes. By advancing our understanding of *TST* and its integration into dialogue systems, my research seeks to contribute to the broader field of human-computer interaction. Through the development of robust and versatile dialogue systems with enhanced style transfer capabilities, we can facilitate more engaging and personalized conversational experiences.

### 1.1 Text Style Transfer

Text style transfer (*TST*) is an NLG task that aims to automatically control the style attributes of a text while preserving the style-independent content (Jin et al., 2022; Hu et al., 2022). In McDonald and Pustejovsky (1985), style is defined as a notion that refers to the manner in which semantics is expressed. Style has also been defined in Hovy (1987) by its pragmatic aspects, which can be expressed as a variety of concepts, such as sentiment, emotion, humor, similes, personality, politeness, formality, simplicity, or authorship, which is generally expressed in the *TST* research as a variety of styles (Jin et al., 2022; Hu et al., 2022). Table 1 shows some basic examples of *TST*.

My research interests in the field of *Text Style Transfer (TST)* encompass several important areas:

- Exploring methods to perform *TST* task without direct supervision (i.e., in case of the unavailability of the parallel data).
- Developing models that accurately control style attributes while preserving the style-independent content in the generated text.
- Deal with the barriers of lack of training and evaluation datasets in *TST* tasks.
- Designing comprehensive evaluation measures tailored specifically to TST tasks to ensure reliable assessments of system performance.
- Build *TST-based* downstream applications.

In my research, I have developed a sentiment transfer model (Mukherjee et al., 2022) that accurately controls sentiment attributes in generated text, striking a balance between style transfer and content preservation. Additionally, I have proposed a polite chatbot (Mukherjee et al., 2023) that generates polite and coherent responses based on the given context.

Moving forward, my future research will focus on further tackling the challenges in TST tasks, introducing innovative automatic evaluation measures, providing benchmark models and datasets for the TST community, and building TST-based applications.

### 1.2 Stylized Dialogue Response Generation

In the field of dialogue systems, researchers are using Text Style Transfer (TST) techniques to generate dialog responses with different styles. TST allows them to manipulate the style of the generated text, such as making it more informal or adding specific emotions or politeness. This enhances the flexibility and adaptability of dialog models to produce text that matches desired style attributes. While traditional research in dialogue response generation focused on producing grammatically correct and contextually relevant responses, it was found that simply being coherent may not make the chatbot engaging.

Politeness plays a crucial role in enhancing interactions and relationships between participants. To address this, we developed a polite chatbot model that generates responses that are both polite and coherent in the given context (Mukherjee et al., 2023).

Researchers also explored generating persona-based responses to maintain consistency and capture background information (Li et al., 2016). They encoded personas of individuals to model human-like behavior. For



*Proceedings of the 19th Annual Meeting of the Young Reseachers' Roundtable on Spoken Dialogue Systems*, pages 44–46
September 11–12, 2023. 

| | **Source Style** | **Target Style** |
|---|---|---|
| Impolite → Polite: | Shut up! the video is starting! | Please be quiet, the video will begin shortly. |
| Negative → Positive: | The food is tasteless. | The food is delicious. |
| Informal → Formal: | The kid is freaking out. | That child is distressed. |

Table 1: *TST* examples regarding sentiment, polarity, and formality.

example, the Emotional Chatting Machine introduced by Zhou et al. (2018) generates responses with emotional tones based on the content.

By leveraging TST techniques and exploring different style attributes, including conversational style, emotion, and politeness, researchers aim to create more engaging and personalized dialog systems. These efforts contribute to aligning dialog systems with user preferences and expectations.

## 2 Spoken dialogue system (SDS) research

In the next 5 to 10 years, the field of dialogue research will witness significant advancements. Young researchers have the opportunity to contribute to transformative developments in Spoken Dialogue Systems (SDS).

The convergence of academia and industry will narrow the gap between theoretical advancements and practical applications. This collaboration will lead to more robust and adaptable SDS architectures, enabling non-experts to create virtual conversational agents and collaborative assistants easily.

Key questions to address include leveraging language models for practical task-oriented dialogue systems, incorporating cognitive modeling to enhance goal-driven behavior, and focusing on user-centricity and extreme personalization.

There are differences between SDS research in academia and industry, with academia emphasizing fully automated learning and interpretability, while industry research gradually incorporates neural components into hand-coded systems.

SDS will be widely used in various scenarios, including voice assistants in everyday devices, specialized applications like car assistants and healthcare, and "AI for good" initiatives for accessibility and inclusivity.

In summary, the future of SDS research lies in the convergence of academia and industry, the development of user-centric and personalized dialogue systems, and collaboration between interdisciplinary researchers.

## 3 Suggested topics for discussion

As we delve into the exciting realm of spoken dialogue systems (SDS) research, we propose three thought-provoking topics for discussion during the event. These topics not only align with our expertise but also resonate with the interests and relevance to the young research community.

**Stylistic Expressiveness in Dialogue Systems:** One area of focus is exploring the potential of text style transfer (TST) in stylized dialog response generation. Discussions can revolve around advancements in generating stylistically expressive responses, including but not limited to polite dialog generation, personalized dialog generation, and other forms of stylized dialog response generation. Sharing best practices, challenges, and novel techniques to achieve high-quality and contextually appropriate stylized responses would enrich our understanding of how to enhance the naturalness and user satisfaction in SDS interactions.

**Evaluation Metrics for Stylized Dialog Systems:** Evaluation plays a crucial role in assessing the effectiveness and performance of SDS, particularly in the context of stylized dialog response generation. Engaging in discussions about the development of evaluation methodologies, metrics, and benchmarks specific to stylistic qualities would greatly benefit the research community. By addressing challenges such as subjective assessment, cross-system comparison, and capturing the nuances of style, we can establish standardized evaluation practices that facilitate fair and comprehensive evaluations of different stylized dialog systems.

**Ethical Considerations in Stylized Dialog Systems:** Given the increasing adoption of SDS and the impact it has on human-computer interactions, ethical considerations are paramount. Engaging in discussions about the ethical implications of stylized dialog systems, such as potential biases, fairness, transparency, and privacy concerns, would enable us to develop responsible and socially aware SDS solutions. By collectively exploring ways to mitigate biases, ensure user privacy, and foster inclusivity in stylized dialog systems, we can shape the future of SDS research with a strong ethical foundation.

These suggested topics provide opportunities for knowledge exchange, critical thinking, and collaboration among researchers interested in text style transfer and stylized dialog response generation. By delving into these areas, we can foster innovation, address challenges, and drive the advancement of SDS technologies with a focus on user-centricity and ethical considerations.

## References

Eduard Hovy. 1987. Generating natural language under pragmatic constraints. *Journal of Pragmatics* 11(6):689–719.

Zhiqiang Hu, Roy Ka-Wei Lee, Charu C Aggarwal, and Aston Zhang. 2022. Text style transfer: A review and experimental evaluation. *ACM SIGKDD Explorations Newsletter* 24(1):14–45.

Di Jin, Zhijing Jin, Zhiting Hu, Olga Vechtomova, and Rada Mihalcea. 2022. Deep learning for text style transfer: A survey. *Computational Linguistics* 48(1):155–205.

Jiwei Li, Michel Galley, Chris Brockett, Georgios P. Spithourakis, Jianfeng Gao, and William B. Dolan. 2016. A persona-based neural conversation model. In *Proceedings of the 54th Annual Meeting of the Association for Computational Linguistics, ACL 2016, August 7-12, 2016, Berlin, Germany, Volume 1: Long Papers*. The Association for Computer Linguistics. https://doi.org/10.18653/v1/p16-1094.

David D McDonald and James Pustejovsky. 1985. A computational theory of prose style for natural language generation. In *Second Conference of the European Chapter of the Association for Computational Linguistics*.

Sourabrata Mukherjee, Vojtěch Hudeček, and Ondřej Dušek. 2023. Polite chatbot: A text style transfer application. In *Proceedings of the 17th Conference of the European Chapter of the Association for Computational Linguistics: Student Research Workshop*. pages 87–93.

Sourabrata Mukherjee, Zdeněk Kasner, and Ondřej Dušek. 2022. Balancing the style-content trade-off in sentiment transfer using polarity-aware denoising. In *International Conference on Text, Speech, and Dialogue*. Springer, pages 172–186.

Hao Zhou, Minlie Huang, Tianyang Zhang, Xiaoyan Zhu, and Bing Liu. 2018. Emotional chatting machine: Emotional conversation generation with internal and external memory. In *AAAI*.

## Biographical sketch

Sourabrata Mukherjee is an aspiring researcher currently pursuing his fourth year of a Ph.D. program at Charles University in the Czech Republic, under the guidance of Ondřej Dušek. Before starting his Ph.D., he worked as a machine learning engineer in the software industry. Sourabrata Mukherjee obtained his master's degree in computer science from the esteemed National Institute of Technology in Durgapur, India.

### 3.1 Acknowledgments

This research was supported by Charles University projects GAUK 392221, SVV 260575, and by the European Research Council (Grant agreement No. 101039303 NG-NLG).

**Mikołaj Krzymiński**

Adam Mickiewicz University
Wieniawskiego 1, 61-712
Poznań, Poland

mikkrz1@st.amu.edu.pl
https://github.com/mikolajkrzyminski/dstc11-track2-intent-induction-data-augmentation

# 1 Research interests

The section is devoted to the author's interests, which are developed in the course of research conducted as part of his development at the university and his professional duties in his paid work.

## 1.1 The process of creating conversational agents

The author's interest is to work on **dialogue systems** and to develop software that will serve a group of users as daily aids within various areas of their lives. As part of his professional experience and research conducted during his graduate study, the author has faced the challenges of producing modern dialog systems. AMUseBot is a system developed as part of a research and development project during the study period. The agent is the user's helper in the process of cooking. The emphasis was placed on the **multimodality** of the system, in addition to the chat interface, the steps of the recipe are presented in an interface, based on a graph, so that the user, can easily follow the steps of the recipe and the agent has a voice interface (Christop et al., 2023).

## 1.2 The NLU part of the conversational agents

The complexity of today's dialogue agents opens the door to many possible studies of individual modules. The author focuses his attention on the NLU module, which is a key component of any dialog system. The responsibility of this module is to understand the current utterances of the user. This task consists of two subtasks, speech act classification, and slot value extraction. The challenges posed are non-trivial, from the fact that the system creators cannot predict what words the user will try to convey information with. There are many techniques used to improve the quality of these modules (Bayer et al., 2021). One of the techniques explored more extensively by the author in his thesis is **data augmentation**. In the thesis, the author focuses on comparing the performance of existing augmentation methods and extending the existing augmentation technique using translation chains within back translation methods.

Aiming to push the boundaries in NLU research, the author announces his work on the challenge announced with the **DSTC11 Track 2** with the title: "Intent Induction from Conversations for Task-Oriented Dialogue". The author tests the impact of the augmentation techniques studied on the final result of the generated solution. The task consists of two subtasks: "**intent clustering**, which requires participants to assign labels to turns in the dialogues where customers express intents **open intent induction**, in which participants must induce a set of intents from dialogues, with each intent defined by a list of sample utterances to be used as training data for an intent classifier." (Gung et al., 2022).

## 1.3 Approach

The adopted solution is to modify only the given datasets, not the clustering algorithm. The text augmentation method is back-translation en->de->en, with the utilization of Opus-MT (Tiedemann and Thottingal, 2020). The particular models are chosen due to the high similarity of the output translations to source data and are being chosen by other authors in similar problems (Ido et al., 2020). The size of the generated set takes values in the range <0.0; 1.0> of the size of the source data.

## 1.4 Results

The results showed an improvement in the performance of the clustering (see 1.4). The induction methods with an accuracy improvement of 4,67% will result in 8th place (among 20 registrations). Achieved results indicate that data augmentation is beneficial to use in unsupervised techniques like in the supervised methods.

| RunID | experiment_id | dataset | F1 | F1_diff |
|---|---|---|---|---|
| glove-840 | dstc11-0.1-s42-a0.4 | test-banking | 37.6549 | +3.4245 |
| all-mpnet | dstc11-0.25-s42-a0.2 | test-banking | 67.9049 | +1.8634 |
| all-mpnet | dstc11-0.5-s42-a0.1 | test-banking | 68.1526 | +0.8859 |
| all-mpnet | dstc11-1.0-s42-a0.075 | test-banking | 68.63 | +2.7782 |
| glove-840 | dstc11-0.1-s42-a0.5 | test-finance | 42.5698 | +12.973 |
| all-mpnet | dstc11-0.25-s42-a0.15 | test-finance | 59.2003 | +5.0649 |
| all-mpnet | dstc11-0.5-s42-a0.5 | test-finance | 59.6556 | +4.527 |
| all-mpnet | dstc11-1.0-s42-a0.1 | test-finance | 59.7538 | -0.9146 |
| all-mpnet | dstc11-0.1-s42-a0.05 | development | 59.7586 | +1.1949 |
| glove-840 | dstc11-0.25-s42-a0.2 | development | 35.7971 | +3.1706 |
| all-mpnet | dstc11-0.5-s42-a0.025 | development | 60.7944 | +7.759 |
| all-mpnet | dstc11-1.0-s42-a0.3 | development | 56.478 | +1.5472 |

experiment_id* - dstc11-<data_size>-s<seed>-a<augmented_size>

Figure 1: Result in f1 metric for augmentation experiments in intent clustering.



*Proceedings of the 19th Annual Meeting of the Young Reseachers' Roundtable on Spoken Dialogue Systems*, pages 47–48
September 11–12, 2023. 

## 2 Spoken dialogue system (SDS) research

Thanks to the recent success and development of LLM and technologies such as ChatGPT (Radford et al., 2019), users are very keen on dialogue systems, and interest in the subject matter and work will bring a number of improvements and enhancements to the technologies we currently know. Although predicting the future of technology for a period of time greater than 5 to 10 years gives the impression of being impossible, there are some fields that are likely to be explored in future works.

- Regarding the growing popularity of virtual agents they will become more accessible and help in more areas of our lives, they will provide legal assistance, health care, and technical assistance.
- The responses of the assistants will be more personalized and will take into account the different contexts of the user, the context of the conversations, the profile of the user, and his mood and emotions.
- More and more optimized solutions will be created, and the computational complexity of the modules used to build the systems will decrease, enabling software developers to start using more and more advanced models to create dialogue assistants (Peng et al., 2023).

## 3 Suggested topics for discussion

Regarding the participation in the DSTC11 challenge and the author's topic of research work, the suggestions for the discussion subjects are:

- The results of the work on the challenge with the DSTC11 in particular: the applied strategy to solve the problem, the results of the used techniques, and the use of augmentation.
- Improvements for the topic of unsupervised augmentation methods, exploration of the subject of back translation, and further directions of research.

The expectations for the dialogue are constantly growing along with the quality of each submodule. The topics presented are particularly important as they relate to improving the quality of the cutting-edge modern NLU module.

## References

Markus Bayer, Marc-André Kaufhold, and Christian Reuter. 2021. A survey on data augmentation for text classification. *CoRR* abs/2107.03158. https://arxiv.org/abs/2107.03158.

Iwona Christop, Kacper Dudzic, and Mikołaj Krzymiński. 2023. Amusebot: Towards making the most out of a task-oriented dialogue system. *Progress in Polish Artificial Intelligence Research* 4, forthcoming.

James Gung, Jason Krone Raphael Shu, Salvatore Romeo, Arshit Gupta, Yassine Benajiba, Saab Mansour, and Yi Zhang. 2022. Dstc11 track proposal: Intent induction from conversations for task-oriented dialogue .

Yuzu Ido, Eunice Yang, and Stephan Sharkov. 2020. Data augmentation with adversarial examples and back-translation.

Bo Peng, Eric Alcaide, Quentin Anthony, Alon Albalak, Samuel Arcadinho, Huanqi Cao, Xin Cheng, Michael Chung, Matteo Grella, Kranthi Kiran GV, Xuzheng He, Haowen Hou, Przemyslaw Kazienko, Jan Kocon, Jiaming Kong, Bartlomiej Koptyra, Hayden Lau, Krishna Sri Ipsit Mantri, Ferdinand Mom, Atsushi Saito, Xiangru Tang, Bolun Wang, Johan S. Wind, Stanislaw Wozniak, Ruichong Zhang, Zhenyuan Zhang, Qihang Zhao, Peng Zhou, Jian Zhu, and Rui-Jie Zhu. 2023. Rwkv: Reinventing rnns for the transformer era.

Alec Radford, Jeff Wu, Rewon Child, David Luan, Dario Amodei, and Ilya Sutskever. 2019. Language models are unsupervised multitask learners.

Jörg Tiedemann and Santhosh Thottingal. 2020. OPUS-MT — Building open translation services for the World. In *Proceedings of the 22nd Annual Conference of the European Association for Machine Translation (EAMT)*. Lisbon, Portugal.

## Biographical sketch

The author's experience with Computer Science began in October 2018 with B.S. studies at Adam Mickiewicz University in Poznań, which ended with the highest grade. The M.Sc. studies in the field of Artificial Intelligence began in February of 2022. The topic of the author's thesis is "Data augmentation methods for dialogue system". Where the results of various data augmentation techniques are being compared and the extensions of existing methods are being presented. During studies, the author had a great possibility to attend numerous multinational conferences and workshops to further explore his knowledge and passion in the domain of NLP. Along with the studies, the author started his professional work as a programmer in November 2021. The author is working on the development of skills for the virtual assistants.

**Adrian Charkiewicz**

Adam Mickiewicz University
Wieniawskiego 1
61-712 Poznań
Poland

adrcha2@st.amu.edu.pl

## 1 Research interests

My research interests encompass two key areas: **measuring user satisfaction** in goal-oriented dialogue systems and exploring the potential of **multi-modal** interactions. In the context of goal-oriented dialogue systems, I am particularly focused on evaluating and enhancing user satisfaction throughout the interaction process. Task-oriented dialogue systems play a vital role in facilitating efficient and effective task completion for users. However, assessing user satisfaction goes beyond simply measuring task success rates and accuracy. It involves capturing the user's subjective perception of satisfaction, which requires the development of comprehensive evaluation methodologies and metrics. I aim to investigate novel approaches for measuring user satisfaction in goal-oriented dialogue systems, addressing the limitations of existing evaluation techniques and proposing innovative strategies for improvement.

Additionally, I am intrigued by the possibilities offered by multi-modal dialogue systems. These systems leverage multiple modes of communication, such as speech, text, gestures, and visuals, to enhance the user experience and improve the overall quality of interactions. By incorporating different modalities, multi-modal dialogue systems have the potential to provide more natural and immersive conversations.

### 1.1 Evaluating user satisfaction in task-oriented dialogue agents

As the field of dialogue agents development continues to advance, it becomes crucial to evaluate their performance and measure user satisfaction. Traditional approaches to evaluating textual documents or tweets may not directly translate to dialogue agents due to the dynamic nature of dialogues and the contextual changes that occur over time (Yang et al., 2022). To ensure user engagement and coherence throughout the conversation, it is important to address the challenges of fulfillment of the user's needs. Additionally, incorporating paralinguistic cues, such as intonation and emotional recognition, can significantly impact the user experience and effectiveness of dialogue agents. I aim to explore different methodologies and approaches for evaluating dialogue agent user satisfaction, considering both subjective and objective measures. By understanding the factors that contribute to user satisfaction, we can enhance the development and deployment of dialogue agent systems to better meet user needs and expectations.

### 1.2 Multimodality in dialogue system

Additionally, my focus extends to the exciting domain of multi-modal dialogue systems, which offer a wide range of possibilities and advancements over traditional text-based solutions. Notably, my team and I have finished developing AMUseBot (Christop et al., 2023), a multi-modal dialogue system designed to assist users in the cooking process. AMUseBot boasts a rich multi-modal interface encompassing speech, text, and dynamic graphs that are presented during conversations. By incorporating multiple modes of communication, AMUseBot creates a more immersive and intuitive user experience, enabling users to interact naturally and obtain information efficiently.

One of the key advantages of multi-modal dialogue agents lies in their ability to leverage different modalities to convey information effectively. While text-based solutions have been predominant in dialogue systems, the inclusion of speech and visual elements adds a new dimension to the interaction, mimicking real-life conversations more closely. With AMUseBot, users can converse through speech, type text, and even receive visual representations of recipes and cooking instructions. This multi-modal approach enhances the system's ability to provide comprehensive assistance and accommodates users with varying preferences or accessibility needs.

Moreover, the architecture of AMUseBot combines both machine-learning and rule-based components, leveraging the strengths of each approach. The machine-learning components enable the system to learn from data and adapt to user preferences, while the rule-based components provide explicit control and enable domain-specific knowledge integration. This hybrid approach ensures the system's flexibility, adaptability, and accuracy in understanding user queries, offering tailored recommendations, and guiding users throughout the process.



*Proceedings of the 19th Annual Meeting of the Young Reseachers' Roundtable on Spoken Dialogue Systems*, pages 49–50
September 11–12, 2023. 

## 2 Spoken dialogue system (SDS) research

- **Where do you think the field of dialogue research will be in 5 to 10 years?** I anticipate a greater emphasis on multi-modal dialogue systems. With advancements in technologies such as Computer Vision and gesture recognition, integrating visual and textual cues into dialogue interactions will provide richer and more immersive experiences. This opens up new possibilities for dialogue systems to understand and respond to not just spoken language but also visual and non-verbal communication, making the interactions more natural and intuitive.

- **What are the most important things for users of SDSs?** SDSs that exhibit context awareness are highly valued. Users expect SDSs to remember the context of the conversation, maintain continuity, and intelligently handle follow-up questions or references. Understanding and retaining contextual information enable SDSs to provide more personalized and relevant responses, enhancing user satisfaction.

- **Will SDSs be more widely used in the future? How? In what scenarios?** While multi-modal dialogue systems contribute to the wider usage of SDSs, their application extends beyond that. SDSs will find extensive use in customer service, healthcare, education, smart homes, and accessibility domains.

- **Is there a difference between SDS research in academia and industry?** Academic researchers delve into fundamental questions, such as dialogue management, state tracking, and user satisfaction metrics, conducting controlled experiments and developing benchmark datasets. In contrast, industry-focused SDS research prioritizes practical applications and real-world deployment, aiming to create commercially viable systems that address user needs and enhance experiences. Industry researchers focus on scalability, robustness, and reliability, optimizing system performance, integration, and engineering considerations.

## 3 Suggested topics for discussion

- Using multimodality in goal-oriented dialogue systems

- Development of robust evaluation metrics for dialogue systems that exhibit a high correlation with human user satisfaction.

- Personalization in dialog. Giving chatbots personas for higher user focus.

## References


Iwona Christop, Kacper Dudzic, and Mikołaj Krzymiński. 2023. Amusebot: Towards making the most out of a task-oriented dialogue system. *Progress in Polish Artificial Intelligence Research 4, forthcoming* .

Deng Yang, Zhang Wenxuan, Lam Wai, Cheng Hong, and Meng Helen. 2022. User satisfaction estimation with sequential dialogue act modeling in goal-oriented conversational systems. *https://aclanthology.org/2022.sigdial-1.59* .


## Biographical sketch

Adrian Charkiewicz is a Computer Science with specialisation in Artificial Inteligence master student at Adam Mickiewicz Univeristy in Poznań. His master thesis is "Modeling user satisfaction in dialogue systems using natural language processing methods". He has experienced working with Natural Language Processing technologies for a company (Poleng) with a team of machine translation researchers.

**Sopan Khosla**

AWS AI Labs
Santa Clara, CA, US

sopankh@amazon.com
https://sopankhosla.github.io/

## 1 Research interests

My research interests broadly lie in the area of **Information Extraction** from Spoken Dialogue, with a spacial focus on **state modeling, anaphora resolution, program synthesis & planning**, and **intent classification** in **goal-oriented conversations**. My aim is to create embedded dialogue systems that can interact with humans in a collaborative setup to solve tasks in a digital/non-digital environment.

Most of the goal-oriented conversations usually involve experts and a laypersons. The aim for the expert is to consider all the information provided by the layperson, identify the underlying set of issues or intents, and prescribe solutions. While human experts are very good at extracting such information, AI agents (that build up most of the automatic dialog systems today) not so much. Most of the existing assistants (or chatbots) only consider individual utterances and do not ground them in the context of the dialogue. My work in this direction has focused on making these systems more effective at extracting the most relevant information from the dialogue to help the human user reach their end-goal.

### 1.1 Information Extraction from Doctor-Patient Dialogue

Following each patient visit, physicians draft long semi-structured clinical summaries called SOAP notes. While invaluable to clinicians and researchers, creating digital SOAP notes is burdensome, contributing to physician burnout. Physicians spend more than 2 hours creating and updating these SOAP notes for every hour of direct patient care.

To automate this arduous task of SOAP note generation, I worked on a pipeline that converts the dialogue into transcripts, performs speaker diarization, extracts the most important utterances from the physician-patient conversation, and then summarizes them in the required format and structure. We built state-of-the-art transformer-based extractive and abstractive summarization architectures to extract the most relevant information from the conversation transcripts (Krishna et al., 2021).

First, the extractive summarization module clusters and classifies the transcript utterances into the SOAP section they contain information for e.g., Past Medical History, Assessment, etc. One of the main novelty points of this module was that it learns contextual representations for each utterance in the conversation by grounding them onto the UMLS (a medical ontology) concepts and conditioning them on the information flow and asymmetric roles/ expertise of the speakers (patient vs physician) (Khosla et al., 2020). Finally, the abstractive module creates a summary for each cluster conditioned on the predicted SOAP note section. This conditioning tailors the output summary to the format expected by each section. Overall, our system was one of the first complete pipelines to automatically generate SOAP notes from conversation transcripts between patients and physicians.

### 1.2 Anaphora Resolution in Dialogue

Most of the earlier work in the Anaphora Resolution community has focused on expository text. Some example datasets include (most domains within) ONTONOTES (Pradhan et al., 2012), GAP (Webster et al., 2018), etc. The systems built on these datasets often focused only on identity anaphora resolution. More recently, research has been carried out for interpretations beyond identity anaphora in datasets like ARRAU (Poesio et al., 2018).

During my Masters, I worked on creating new benchmarks and systems for three types of anaphoric relations (identity, bridging, discourse deixis) in a dialogue setting. I spearheaded the creation of multiple dialogue datasets labeled with these different types of anaphoric relations. These datasets were then used to host the CODI-CRAC 2021 (Khosla et al., 2021) and 2022 (Yu et al., 2022a) Shared-tasks where we invited other researchers in the community to build new systems that solve this problem. I also worked on the metrics that were used to score the different systems that were submitted to the shared task (Yu et al., 2022b). We created a first of its kind state-of-the-art benchmark dataset, and a baseline system to perform automatic resolution of these three different types of anaphoric relationships in dialogue. Our system was built on top of a transformer-based encoding layer, trained, and evaluated to perform generalizable anaphora resolution in different types of dialogue settings.

### 1.3 Intent Classification in Dialogue

My ongoing work is in performing contextual intent classification in spoken & written dialogue between humans and an agent. Most of the existing production-ready as-



*Proceedings of the 19th Annual Meeting of the Young Reseachers' Roundtable on Spoken Dialogue Systems*, pages 51–53
September 11–12, 2023. 

sistants are not good at grounding the interactions in the context of the dialogue.

I am actively researching on creating dialogue systems that can perform context-dependent intent classification on the incoming user utterance, and interact with external tools/ APIs to perform further processing conditioned on that intent. I worked on a transformer-based state-of-the-art intent classification system that not only classifies incoming utterances into different intents that the assistant can handle, but also detect utterances that are out-of-scope for the assistant's current capabilities to gracefully convey to the customer (Khosla and Gangadharaiah, 2022b). In our recent work, we also created a new intent-classification dataset that evaluates the prowess of state-of-the-art models on samples that can prove to be adversarial in the production scenario Khosla and Gangadharaiah (2022a). The dataset was a significant contribution as it was a first of its kind that evaluated intent classification systems on non-iid distributions.

## 2 Spoken dialogue system (SDS) research

Owing to the fast-paced innovations in language and speech, SDSs are likely to transition into becoming useful assistants for the human users. They might go one step further, and be able to interact with their environment to perform tasks and help the user achieve their goal. To get to this stage, however, SDS research has to focus on dialog management modules that are capable of accurately modeling user's intents and goals, translating those intents into actionable steps (or programs), executing those steps in their (digital) environment, and deploying remedial measures when needed. All of which will need to happen in a transparent, verifiable, and controlled setting.

## 3 Suggested topics for discussion

- End-to-end vs Modular methodologies for Spoken Dialogue Assistants.
- Program Synthesis and Planning in Dialogue Assistants to perform complex tasks.
- Methods for Efficient Interaction with Digital/Non Digital APIs and Tools.
- Modeling multi-modal context in Dialogue.

## References


Sopan Khosla and Rashmi Gangadharaiah. 2022a. Benchmarking the covariate shift robustness of open-world intent classification approaches. In *Proceedings of the 2nd Conference of the Asia-Pacific Chapter of the Association for Computational Linguistics and the 12th International Joint Conference on Natural Language Processing (Volume 2: Short Papers)*. Association for Computational Linguistics, Online only, pages 14–23. https://aclanthology.org/2022.aacl-short.3.

Sopan Khosla and Rashmi Gangadharaiah. 2022b. Evaluating the practical utility of confidence-score based techniques for unsupervised open-world classification. In *Proceedings of the Third Workshop on Insights from Negative Results in NLP*. Association for Computational Linguistics, Dublin, Ireland, pages 18–23. https://doi.org/10.18653/v1/2022.insights-1.3.

Sopan Khosla, Shikhar Vashishth, Jill Fain Lehman, and Carolyn Rose. 2020. MedFilter: Improving Extraction of Task-relevant Utterances through Integration of Discourse Structure and Ontological Knowledge. In *Proceedings of the 2020 Conference on Empirical Methods in Natural Language Processing (EMNLP)*. Association for Computational Linguistics, Online, pages 7781–7797. https://doi.org/10.18653/v1/2020.emnlp-main.626.

Sopan Khosla, Juntao Yu, Ramesh Manuvinakurike, Vincent Ng, Massimo Poesio, Michael Strube, and Carolyn Rosé. 2021. The CODI-CRAC 2021 shared task on anaphora, bridging, and discourse deixis in dialogue. In *Proceedings of the CODI-CRAC 2021 Shared Task on Anaphora, Bridging, and Discourse Deixis in Dialogue*. Association for Computational Linguistics, Punta Cana, Dominican Republic, pages 1–15. https://doi.org/10.18653/v1/2021.codi-sharedtask.1.

Kundan Krishna, Sopan Khosla, Jeffrey Bigham, and Zachary C. Lipton. 2021. Generating SOAP notes from doctor-patient conversations using modular summarization techniques. In *Proceedings of the 59th Annual Meeting of the Association for Computational Linguistics and the 11th International Joint Conference on Natural Language Processing (Volume 1: Long Papers)*. Association for Computational Linguistics, Online, pages 4958–4972. https://doi.org/10.18653/v1/2021.acl-long.384.

Massimo Poesio, Yulia Grishina, Varada Kolhatkar, Nafise Moosavi, Ina Roesiger, Adam Roussel, Fabian Simonjetz, Alexandra Uma, Olga Uryupina, Juntao Yu, and Heike Zinsmeister. 2018. Anaphora resolution with the ARRAU corpus. In *Proceedings of the First Workshop on Computational Models of Reference, Anaphora and Coreference*. Association for Computational Linguistics, New Orleans, Louisiana, pages 11–22. https://doi.org/10.18653/v1/W18-0702.

Sameer Pradhan, Alessandro Moschitti, Nianwen Xue, Olga Uryupina, and Yuchen Zhang. 2012. CoNLL-2012 shared task: Modeling multilingual unrestricted coreference in OntoNotes. In *Joint Conference on*

*EMNLP and CoNLL - Shared Task*. Association for Computational Linguistics, Jeju Island, Korea, pages 1–40. https://aclanthology.org/W12-4501.

Kellie Webster, Marta Recasens, Vera Axelrod, and Jason Baldridge. 2018. Mind the GAP: A balanced corpus of gendered ambiguous pronouns. *Transactions of the Association for Computational Linguistics* 6:605–617. https://doi.org/10.1162/tacl$_{a0}$0240.

Juntao Yu, Sopan Khosla, Ramesh Manuvinakurike, Lori Levin, Vincent Ng, Massimo Poesio, Michael Strube, and Carolyn Rosé. 2022a. The CODI-CRAC 2022 shared task on anaphora, bridging, and discourse deixis in dialogue. In *Proceedings of the CODI-CRAC 2022 Shared Task on Anaphora, Bridging, and Discourse Deixis in Dialogue*. Association for Computational Linguistics, Gyeongju, Republic of Korea, pages 1–14. https://aclanthology.org/2022.codi-crac.1.

Juntao Yu, Sopan Khosla, Nafise Sadat Moosavi, Silviu Paun, Sameer Pradhan, and Massimo Poesio. 2022b. The universal anaphora scorer. In *Proceedings of the Thirteenth Language Resources and Evaluation Conference*. European Language Resources Association, Marseille, France, pages 4873–4883. https://aclanthology.org/2022.lrec-1.521.

## Biographical sketch

Sopan Khosla is an Applied Scientist at AWS AI Labs. His research focuses on Information Extraction from Spoken Dialogue, with a spacial focus on state modeling, anaphora resolution, program synthesis & planning, and intent classification in goal-oriented conversations. He holds a Masters degree in Language Technologies from Carnegie Mellon University, where he was advised by Prof. Carolyn Rose. During his masters, he worked on problems relating to anaphora resolution, discourse modeling, and knowledge grounding in dialogues. In his free time, he enjoys playing Badminton and Tennis.

Shutong Feng

Heinrich Heine University Düsseldorf
Universitätsstraße 1
40225 Düsseldorf
Germany

shutong.feng@hhu.de
https://shutongfeng.github.io/

## 1 Research interests

My research interests lie in the area of **modelling natural and human-like conversations**, with a special focus on **emotions in task-oriented dialogue (ToD) systems**. ToD systems need to produce semantically and grammatically correct responses to fulfil the user's goal. Being able to perceive and express emotions pushes them one more step towards achieving human-likeness. To begin with, I constructed a dataset with meaningful emotion labels as well as a wide coverage of emotions and linguistic features in ToDs. Then, I improved emotion recognition in conversations (ERC) in the task-oriented domain by exploiting key characteristics of ToDs. Currently, I am working towards enhancing ToD systems with emotions.

### 1.1 Dataset Construction

Current research on emotions in conversations focuses on chit-chat dialogues because chit-chat dialogues are means for emotional expression and therefore are usually rich in emotions. Yet, emotions in ToDs, another important genre of spoken dialogues, are overlooked. In ToDs, users aim to achieve specific goals, such as hotel booking, by interacting with the system. While it is true that users do not express emotion the same way as they do in chit-chat dialogues, I observed that users do express various emotions concerning their goals. Users may talk about their feelings towards assorted situations that prompt them to interact with the system, such as a robbery or a vacation. It is also not uncommon to observe that users apologise to the system when they believe that they have caused trouble or confusion to the system, for example, when they try to correct or change their search criteria. In some worse scenarios, users may even insult the system. I am interested in such emotional nuances in users, which can have different implications for the system and would require different response strategies. This led me to construct **EmoWOZ, a corpus of task-oriented dialogues** where user emotions are annotated with our **tailored annotation scheme** (Feng et al., 2022).

#### 1.1.1 Annotation Scheme for User Emotions

Existing ERC datasets make use of basic emotions from psychological theories. However, these emotion labels do not capture enough emotional nuances that are meaningful enough for ToDs. For example, to a ToD agent, it is unclear what "happiness" or "positive" means. What is missing that may influence system response here is whether the user emotion is elicited by the system.

In this spirit, I designed a tailored annotation scheme inspired by the Ortony, Collins, and Clore (OCC) model where emotions are defined as valenced reactions to various cognitive elicitors (Ortony et al., 1988). I devised a set of seven emotion labels considering three emotional aspects: **valence, elicitor, and conduct**. Valence concerns the positivity or negativity of emotions. Elicitor can be the system, including the entity proposed by the system, an event/fact, which is out of control of the system, or the user. The conduct aspect accounts for abusive behaviours.

#### 1.1.2 Dialogue Collection and Annotation

I annotated user emotions in dialogues from two sources using Amazon Mechanical Turk. The first source is **MultiWOZ** (Budzianowski et al., 2018), one of the most well-established datasets for ToD modelling. Existing dialogue state labels in MultiWOZ allow us to investigate how task information can be leveraged to improve emotion recognition. The numerous benchmark results on MultiWOZ also allow us to directly assess the effectiveness of introducing emotion in ToD modelling tasks.

Since dialogues in MultiWOZ are human-to-human, and human operators rarely make mistakes, I additionally collected human-to-machine dialogues for balanced emotion coverage and diverse linguistic expressions. We refer to this sub-set as **DialMAGE** (**Dia**logues with a **MA**chine **GE**nerated policy).

#### 1.1.3 Annotation Quality Assurance

Given the difficulty and subjectivity in text emotion annotation, we adopted several quality assurance methods such as tutorials, qualification tests, hidden tests, and outlier detection. Each utterance was annotated by three English-speaking workers. The final inter-annotator agreement (Fleiss' Kappa) is 0.6, suggesting moderate to substantial agreement. This suggests a good usability of the dataset.



*Proceedings of the 19th Annual Meeting of the Young Reseachers' Roundtable on Spoken Dialogue Systems*, pages 54–56
September 11–12, 2023. 

### 1.2 Improving ERC in ToDs

To build an emotion-aware ToD system, the first step is to give the system the ability to recognise user emotions. I first trained chit-chat ERC models with EmoWOZ and observed suboptimal results. This motivated me to exploit the characteristics of ToDs to improve ERC in ToDs. I proposed a framework called **ERToD** (**E**motion **R**ecogniser for **T**ask-**o**riented **D**ialogues), which effectively adapts chit-chat ERC models to the task-oriented domain by addressing three critical aspects: data, features, and objectives. First, I proposed two strategies of data augmentation to alleviate the class imbalance in EmoWOZ. Second, I used dialogue state as the task information encoding in combination with sentiment-aware text encoding. Third, I devised a multi-task learning objective and a novel emotion-distance weighted loss function. These approaches significantly improved the ERC performance of existing models.

### 1.3 Enhancing ToD Systems with Emotion

The ultimate goal of studying emotions in ToDs is to improve the system in either objective evaluation metrics or subjective user experience. Emotion is very important for a human operator, so can it influence all components in a modular ToD system. Correctly identifying the user emotion by the operator helps accurately identify the intent of the user and the status of the task completion, suggesting the potential of using emotion to improve downstream ToD modelling.

I showed that by considering emotion recognition as an auxiliary task in a multi-task learning framework, the joint goal accuracy of TripPy (Heck et al., 2020), a strong BERT-based dialogue state tracker, can be significantly improved. Our group has also developed an emotional user simulator (Lin et al., 2023), which exhibits diverse emotional expressions while achieving comparable task-related performance with other state-of-the-art generative user simulators. Currently, I am working towards incorporating emotion into other ToD modules, namely the dialogue policy and the natural language generator.

## 2 Spoken dialogue system (SDS) research

I expect in the future that SDSs can be more human-like by not only mimicking human responses but also mimicking the thinking process of humans. This should involve rationalising each decision of the system. Specific to my research interest, I envisage more use of emotion in task-oriented dialogue systems to push further the system performance as well as to improve the explainability of system behaviours via emotion. For example, the system should understand the user's situation and the cause of the user's emotion, which can hopefully lead to an optimal choice of dialogue acts as well as the system's emotional conduct.

## 3 Suggested topics for discussion

- **Ethics in Conversational AI:** When talking to computers, users are less refrained from showing impoliteness. What can we do to detect such behaviours? What is the proper response of a conversational AI? How can a conversational AI redirect the user towards good conduct?
- **Professionality:** What is the desired interpersonal skill and emotional behaviour of a ToD agent when it tries to show empathy?
- **Large Language Models (LLMs):** How can LLMs be applied to ToD when they are still prone to problems such as confabulation?

## Biographical sketch

Shutong Feng is a third-year PhD student at the Chair for Dialog System and Machine Learning, Heinrich Heine University Düsseldorf. He is supervised by Prof. Dr. Milica Gašić and co-supervised by Dr. Nurul Lubis. He is interested in modelling human-like ToD systems. Shutong obtained his BA and MEng degrees from the University of Cambridge in 2019. He then worked as an engineer at Huawei before starting his PhD study in 2020.

## References


Paweł Budzianowski, Tsung-Hsien Wen, Bo-Hsiang Tseng, Iñigo Casanueva, Stefan Ultes, Osman Ramadan, and Milica Gašić. 2018. MultiWOZ - a large-scale multi-domain Wizard-of-Oz dataset for task-oriented dialogue modelling. In *Proceedings of the 2018 Conference on Empirical Methods in Natural Language Processing*. Association for Computational Linguistics, Brussels, Belgium, pages 5016–5026. https://doi.org/10.18653/v1/D18-1547.

Shutong Feng, Nurul Lubis, Christian Geishauser, Hsien-chin Lin, Michael Heck, Carel van Niekerk, and Milica Gasic. 2022. EmoWOZ: A large-scale corpus and labelling scheme for emotion recognition in task-oriented dialogue systems. In *Proceedings of the Thirteenth Language Resources and Evaluation Conference*. European Language Resources Association, Marseille, France, pages 4096–4113. https://aclanthology.org/2022.lrec-1.436.

Michael Heck, Carel van Niekerk, Nurul Lubis, Christian Geishauser, Hsien-Chin Lin, Marco Moresi, and Milica Gasic. 2020. TripPy: A triple copy strategy for value independent neural dialog state tracking. In *Proceedings of the 21th Annual Meeting of the Special Interest Group on Discourse and Dialogue*. Association for Computational Linguistics, 1st virtual meeting, pages 35–44. https://aclanthology.org/2020.sigdial-1.4.

Hsien-Chin Lin, Shutong Feng, Christian Geishauser, Nurul Lubis, Carel van Niekerk, Michael Heck, Benjamin Ruppik, Renato Vukovic, and Milica Gasic. 2023. Emous: Simulating user emotions in task-oriented dialogues.

Andrew Ortony, Gerald L. Clore, and Allan Collins. 1988. *The Cognitive Structure of Emotions*. Cambridge University Press. https://doi.org/10.1017/CBO9780511571299.

# Brielen Madureira

University of Potsdam
Karl-Liebknecht-Straße 24-25
14476 Potsdam
Germany

madureiralasota@uni-potsdam.de
https://www.ling.uni-potsdam.de/~madureiralasota/


## 1 Research interests

I am broadly interested in **evaluation** of dialogue systems, in all its many facets: The data they are trained on, their ability to perform a task successfully, their skills with respect to various dialogue phenomena, their resemblance to human cognitive processes, and their ethical and societal impact. More specifically, my research topics focus on understanding the possibilities and limits of current multimodal neural network-based models to incrementally encode information for natural language understanding in general and also for **building common ground** and **asking for clarification**. Besides, I am interested in **dialogue games** as a means to elicit and collect dialogue data and to evaluate the abilities of dialogue models.

### 1.1 Incremental Processing in the Age of Non-Incremental Encoders

My main line of research has been on employing bidirectional models, like bidirectional LSTMs (Hochreiter and Schmidhuber, 1997) and Transformers (Vaswani et al., 2017), for **incremental processing**. When used under a restart-incremental paradigm (Schlangen and Skantze, 2011), these models incrementally build partial representations that are useful despite they typically being trained on full sequences. I have assessed their incremental behaviour on multiple tasks (Madureira and Schlangen, 2020; Kahardipraja et al., 2021). Then, I supervised a thesis on modelling a recomputation policy (Kahardipraja et al., 2023), which led to a proposal of an **evaluation methodology for revisions** (to be presented at SIGdial 2023). I am currently interested in finding means to interpret these sequences of partial hypotheses, linguistically and with the aid of cognitively-motivated signals.

### 1.2 Scorekeeping

Beyond token-level incremental processing, dialogue models should handle the **conversational grounding** turn by turn, incrementally building representations that encode what information is private and at which moment something becomes (and remains) shared. I have proposed an evaluation method (Madureira and Schlangen, 2022) to investigate to what degree visual dialogue models appropriately do **scorekeeping** (Lewis, 1979). This method has been realised both as a probing task with the internal state representations and also by posing direct questions to an agent.

### 1.3 Clarification Requests in Multimodal Dialogue Games

Dialogue games can be useful means both to collect dialogue data and to evaluate a dialogue model. I have been studying the **multimodal, instruction-following** CoDraw game (Kim et al., 2019) in more detail, and have provided annotation on **Instruction Clarification Requests** which shows that this is a very rich and large CR dataset (Madureira and Schlangen, 2023b,a). I have been working on the task of detecting the moments to ask iCRs and am also interested in the problems of *what* and *how* to ask.

## 2 Spoken dialogue system (SDS) research

I do not dare trying to predict what the field of dialogue research will be in 5 to 10 years given the pace of the latest innovations. But I am convinced that evaluation is a cornerstone for model development and deployment, and that evaluation has to be much more than optimising metrics. We need evaluation for transparency, for policy making, for increasing the literacy and awareness of users interacting with SDS. I strongly support that everyone involved in building SDS continuously seek to sharpen their perspectives on our responsibility, as individuals and as a community, also beyond the technical and theoretical aspects. We need opportunities to promote and take part in *dialogues* on many urgent topics, for instance: The impact of these technologies in the world, the protection of vulnerable groups, the options for regulation, the mitigation of risks, the influence of commercial interests on research and on users, and the power concentration. I am interested in discussing what *actions* can or should be taken and what should we really be aiming for when building or evaluating SDS.



*Proceedings of the 19th Annual Meeting of the Young Reseachers' Roundtable on Spoken Dialogue Systems*, pages 57–58
September 11–12, 2023. ©2023 Association for Computational Linguistics

## 3 Suggested topics for discussion

- Modelling decisions token by token or turn by turn, when the signal is sparse.
- Limitations of crowdworking as a method for data collection and evaluation. Impact of task instructions, misunderstandings, subjective judgements, quality of the data.
- Ethical considerations of what can be done *versus* what should be done.

## References


Sepp Hochreiter and Jürgen Schmidhuber. 1997. Long short-term memory. *Neural Comput.* 9(8):1735–1780. https://doi.org/10.1162/neco.1997.9.8.1735.

Patrick Kahardipraja, Brielen Madureira, and David Schlangen. 2021. Towards incremental transformers: An empirical analysis of transformer models for incremental NLU. In *Proceedings of the 2021 Conference on Empirical Methods in Natural Language Processing*. Association for Computational Linguistics, Online and Punta Cana, Dominican Republic, pages 1178–1189. https://doi.org/10.18653/v1/2021.emnlp-main.90.

Patrick Kahardipraja, Brielen Madureira, and David Schlangen. 2023. TAPIR: Learning adaptive revision for incremental natural language understanding with a two-pass model. In *Findings of the Association for Computational Linguistics: ACL 2023*. Association for Computational Linguistics, Toronto, Canada, pages 4173–4197. https://aclanthology.org/2023.findings-acl.257.

Jin-Hwa Kim, Nikita Kitaev, Xinlei Chen, Marcus Rohrbach, Byoung-Tak Zhang, Yuandong Tian, Dhruv Batra, and Devi Parikh. 2019. CoDraw: Collaborative drawing as a testbed for grounded goal-driven communication. In *Proceedings of the 57th Annual Meeting of the Association for Computational Linguistics*. Association for Computational Linguistics, Florence, Italy, pages 6495–6513. https://doi.org/10.18653/v1/P19-1651.

David Lewis. 1979. Scorekeeping in a language game. In *Semantics from different points of view*, Springer, pages 172–187.

Brielen Madureira and David Schlangen. 2020. Incremental processing in the age of non-incremental encoders: An empirical assessment of bidirectional models for incremental NLU. In *Proceedings of the 2020 Conference on Empirical Methods in Natural Language Processing (EMNLP)*. Association for Computational Linguistics, Online, pages 357–374. https://doi.org/10.18653/v1/2020.emnlp-main.26.

Brielen Madureira and David Schlangen. 2022. Can visual dialogue models do scorekeeping? exploring how dialogue representations incrementally encode shared knowledge. In *Proceedings of the 60th Annual Meeting of the Association for Computational Linguistics (Volume 2: Short Papers)*. Association for Computational Linguistics, Dublin, Ireland, pages 651–664. https://doi.org/10.18653/v1/2022.acl-short.73.

Brielen Madureira and David Schlangen. 2023a. "are you telling me to put glasses on the dog?" content-grounded annotation of instruction clarification requests in the codraw dataset.

Brielen Madureira and David Schlangen. 2023b. Instruction clarification requests in multimodal collaborative dialogue games: Tasks, and an analysis of the CoDraw dataset. In *Proceedings of the 17th Conference of the European Chapter of the Association for Computational Linguistics*. Association for Computational Linguistics, Dubrovnik, Croatia, pages 2303–2319. https://aclanthology.org/2023.eacl-main.169.

David Schlangen and Gabriel Skantze. 2011. A General, Abstract Model of Incremental Dialogue Processing. *Dialogue and Discourse* 2(1):83–111. https://doi.org/10.5087/dad.2011.105.

Ashish Vaswani, Noam Shazeer, Niki Parmar, Jakob Uszkoreit, Llion Jones, Aidan N Gomez, Łukasz Kaiser, and Illia Polosukhin. 2017. Attention is all you need. *Advances in neural information processing systems* 30.


## Biographical sketch

Brielen Madureira is a fourth-year Ph.D. student at the Computational Linguistics Lab in the University of Potsdam, Germany, being supervised by Prof. David Schlangen. She holds a M.Sc. degree in Language Science and Technology from the University of Saarland, Germany, and a B.Sc. in Applied and Computational Mathematics from the University of São Paulo, Brazil. She has helped create the group Brazilian Women in NLP and organise the Student Research Workshop at ACL 2022. When she is not working towards graduating, she can often be found bird watching (📷 🐦) and admiring nature (🌳 🌻 🏞️).

**Ye Liu**

Mercedes-Benz AG & Ulm University
Benz-Straße
71063 Sindelfingen
Germany

ye.y.liu@mercedes-benz.com

## 1 Research interests

My research work centers on how to enable a human-like interaction through generating contextual, emotional or proactive responses, both in task-oriented and in chit-chat spoken dialogue systems (SDSs), because natural language generation (NLG) is an indispensable component in SDSs and can directly affect the user interactive experience of the entire dialogue system. In addition to NLG, I am also interested in natural language understanding (NLU), as it plays a crucial role in SDSs and is a prerequisite for dialogue systems to generate replies.

### 1.1 Commonsense enabled conversational model

Many pre-trained transformer-based (Vaswani et al., 2017) language models (LMs) have been widely applied in SDSs and shown promising performance. However, the probing experiments in Zhou et al. (2021) demonstrated that pre-trained LMs (Zhang et al., 2020; Roller et al., 2021; Lewis et al., 2020) fail to capture commonsense (CS) knowledge hidden in dialogue utterances, even though they were already pre-trained with numerous datasets.

To improve the CS understanding and reasoning ability of a pre-trained model and to build a dialogue agent like shown in Figure 1, we firstly inject external knowledge into a pre-trained conversational model to establish basic commonsense. Secondly, we leverage this integrated commonsense capability to improve open-domain dialogue response generation so that the dialogue agent is capable of understanding the CS knowledge hidden in dialogue history on top of inferring related other knowledge to further guide response generation (Liu et al., 2022a).

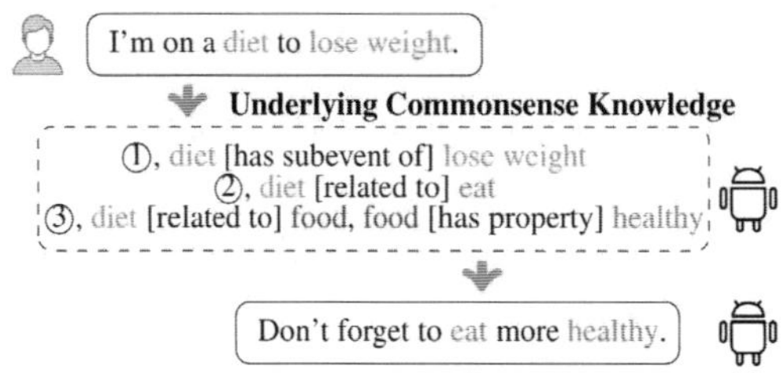


Figure 1: The ideal dialogue agent can understand the CS knowledge hidden in the dialogue history (①), meanwhile, infer the reasonable CS knowledge (② and ③) for further guiding an informative response generation.

### 1.2 System-initiated transitions in unified SDSs

SDSs have been separately developed under two different categories, task-oriented and chit-chat. The former focuses on achieving functional goals and the latter aims at creating engaging social conversations without special goals. Creating a unified conversational model that can engage in both chit-chat and task-oriented dialogues is a promising research topic in recent years. We investigate the "initiative" that occurs when there is a transition from chit-chat to task-oriented in one dialogue and develop proactive capabilities for unified models to be able to initiate this transition through generating a transition sentence (Liu et al., 2023b).

We firstly build a *transition info extractor* (TIE) that keeps track of the preceding chit-chat interaction and detects the potential user intention to switch to a task-oriented service. Meanwhile, in the unified model, a *transition sentence generator* (TSG) is extended through efficient Adapter tuning and transition prompt learning. When the TIE successfully finds task-related information from the preceding chit-chat, such as a transition domain ("train") or transition value ("London Kings Cross"), then the TSG is activated automatically in the unified model to initiate this transition by generating a transition sentence under the guidance of transition information extracted by TIE (like "If you want, I can look for a train to London Kings Cross for you."). This proactivity is beneficial for commercial dialogue systems to actively sell their task-related services (Chiu et al., 2022; Liu et al., 2022b).

## 2 Spoken dialogue system (SDS) research

- **How to tackle hallucinations in large generative models, such as ChatGPT?** Compared with its predecessors, like GPT-2, the ChatGPT improved ability to generate more reasonable replies in various



*Proceedings of the 19th Annual Meeting of the Young Reseachers' Roundtable on Spoken Dialogue Systems*, pages 59–61
September 11–12, 2023. 

contexts. However, it is difficult to completely eliminate the hallucinating generations even with ChatGPT or GPT-4, especially when dealing with complex topics. In the future, reducing hallucinations effectively might be a persistent challenge, as it is related to the inherent properties of neural network architectures. In addition to model development, we can apply some post-processing technologies to identify and remove hallucinations from the generated output.

- **How to enhance LLMs with knowledge graphs (KGs)?** Along with the introduction of LLMs, people are more interested in integrating external knowledge, such as knowledge graphs (KGs), into LLMs to enhance its performance, especially for fact-aware or question answering (QA) tasks. Yang et al. (2023) provides a comprehensive review for KGs enhanced pre-trained LMs and proposes some possible research directions. From my perspective, it is crucial to consider how KGs can be incorporated into dialogue-based generative models. Given the impressive performance of ChatGPT, it is worth to explore to what extent external knowledge can be effectively exploited.

## 3 Suggested topics for discussion

I suggest discussing the following topics:

- **Chances and challenges to SDS research community along with the launch of ChatGPT:** Since its release at the end of 2022, ChatGPT has received significant attention from both industry and academia. This surge of interest has led to a growing number of researcher to devote themselves into the study of large language models (LLMs). Meanwhile, we have also witnessed many surprising and amazing applications for these models, such as Microsoft 365 Copilot. Despite the promising opportunities, young researchers also encounter various challenges. Because a series of ChatGPT and GPT-4 models are no longer publicly available, they are not easily accessible to young researcher. Even if we have access, do we have sufficient computing resources to run these LLMs? On the other hand, there is a need to reconsider the development of SDS, such as for emotional chatbot, we previously explicitly predict emotions in user utterances and leverage this information to enable empathetic responses. However, the question arises now if it is necessary to put in the effort to explicitly detect user emotions and improve the accuracy of emotion detection. Because with advanced capabilities, ChatGPT have demonstrated the ability to perceive user emotions and generate appropriate responses accordingly (Elyoseph et al., 2023) even without predicting user emotions.

- **Understanding ability of ChatGPT:** ChatGPT and its predecessor GPT-2 are both auto-regressive generation models. However, the ChatGPT has shown impressive capability in understanding a wide range of topics, which underlies its remarkable performance on generating human-like responses. Some academic studies have started to investigate and evaluate the logical reasoning ability of ChatGPT and GPT-4 (Liu et al., 2023a; Zhong et al., 2023; Zhao et al., 2023). Hence, there are some follow-up questions, like how can we accurately evaluate the understanding ability of these large generative models? Furthermore, do we underestimate the performance of these large generative models in terms of its understanding ability?

- **Evaluation in LLMs:** To assess the performance of LLMs, many researchers subject ChatGPT to various Benchmarks (Zhong et al., 2023; Bang et al., 2023). Zhao et al. (2023) explores the emotional dialogue capabilities in ChatGPT and finds that metric results may not necessarily reflect its poor understanding. One potential reason is significant discrepancy between its prediction standard and annotation standard. When it comes to generation tasks, human evaluation is commonly viewed as the best reliable way to evaluate NLG systems, but come with many issues, such as costly and time consuming and human judgement bias (Celikyilmaz et al., 2020). However, some papers (Chiang and Lee, 2023) investigate the possibility of using LLMs to be an alternative to human evaluation.

## References


Yejin Bang, Samuel Cahyawijaya, Nayeon Lee, Wenliang Dai, Dan Su, Bryan Wilie, Holy Lovenia, Ziwei Ji, Tiezheng Yu, Willy Chung, et al. 2023. A multitask, multilingual, multimodal evaluation of chatgpt on reasoning, hallucination, and interactivity. *arXiv preprint arXiv:2302.04023* .

Asli Celikyilmaz, Elizabeth Clark, and Jianfeng Gao. 2020. Evaluation of text generation: A survey. *arXiv preprint arXiv:2006.14799* .

Cheng-Han Chiang and Hung-yi Lee. 2023. Can large language models be an alternative to human evaluations? *arXiv preprint arXiv:2305.01937* .

Ssu Chiu, Maolin Li, Yen-Ting Lin, and Yun-Nung Chen. 2022. Salesbot: Transitioning from chit-chat to task-oriented dialogues. In *Proceedings of the 60th Annual Meeting of the Association for Computational Linguistics (Volume 1: Long Papers)*. pages 6143–6158.

Zohar Elyoseph, Dorit Hadar-Shoval, Kfir Asraf, and Maya Lvovsky. 2023. Chatgpt outperforms humans in emotional awareness evaluations. *Frontiers in Psychology* 14:1199058.

Mike Lewis, Yinhan Liu, Naman Goyal, Marjan Ghazvininejad, Abdelrahman Mohamed, Omer Levy, Veselin Stoyanov, and Luke Zettlemoyer. 2020. Bart: Denoising sequence-to-sequence pre-training for natural language generation, translation, and comprehension. In *Proceedings of the 58th Annual Meeting of the Association for Computational Linguistics*. pages 7871–7880.

Hanmeng Liu, Ruoxi Ning, Zhiyang Teng, Jian Liu, Qiji Zhou, and Yue Zhang. 2023a. Evaluating the logical reasoning ability of chatgpt and gpt-4. *arXiv preprint arXiv:2304.03439* .

Ye Liu, Wolfgang Maier, Wolfgang Minker, and Stefan Ultes. 2022a. Conceptnet infused dialogpt for underlying commonsense understanding and reasoning in dialogue response generation. In *Proceedings of the 26th Workshop on the Semantics and Pragmatics of Dialogue - Poster Abstracts*. SEMDIAL, Dublin, Ireland.

Ye Liu, Stefan Ultes, Wolfgang Minker, and Wolfgang Maier. 2023b. Unified conversational models with system-initiated transitions between chit-chat and task-oriented dialogues. *arXiv preprint arXiv:2307.01664* .

Ye Liu, Yung-Ching Yang, Wolfgang Maier, Wolfgang Minker, and Stefan Ultes. 2022b. On system-initiated transitions in a unified natural language generation model for dialogue systems. In *Proceedings of the 26th Workshop on the Semantics and Pragmatics of Dialogue - Poster Abstracts*. SEMDIAL, Dublin, Ireland.

Stephen Roller, Emily Dinan, Naman Goyal, Da Ju, Mary Williamson, Yinhan Liu, Jing Xu, Myle Ott, Eric Michael Smith, Y-Lan Boureau, et al. 2021. Recipes for building an open-domain chatbot. In *Proceedings of the 16th Conference of the European Chapter of the Association for Computational Linguistics: Main Volume*. pages 300–325.

Ashish Vaswani, Noam Shazeer, Niki Parmar, Jakob Uszkoreit, Llion Jones, Aidan N Gomez, Łukasz Kaiser, and Illia Polosukhin. 2017. Attention is all you need. *Advances in neural information processing systems* 30.

Linyao Yang, Hongyang Chen, Zhao Li, Xiao Ding, and Xindong Wu. 2023. Chatgpt is not enough: Enhancing large language models with knowledge graphs for fact-aware language modeling. *arXiv preprint arXiv:2306.11489* .

Yizhe Zhang, Siqi Sun, Michel Galley, Yen-Chun Chen, Chris Brockett, Xiang Gao, Jianfeng Gao, Jingjing Liu, and William B Dolan. 2020. Dialogpt: Large-scale generative pre-training for conversational response generation. In *Proceedings of the 58th Annual Meeting of the Association for Computational Linguistics: System Demonstrations*. pages 270–278.

Weixiang Zhao, Yanyan Zhao, Xin Lu, Shilong Wang, Yanpeng Tong, and Bing Qin. 2023. Is chatgpt equipped with emotional dialogue capabilities? *arXiv preprint arXiv:2304.09582* .

Qihuang Zhong, Liang Ding, Juhua Liu, Bo Du, and Dacheng Tao. 2023. Can chatgpt understand too? a comparative study on chatgpt and fine-tuned bert. *arXiv preprint arXiv:2302.10198* .

Pei Zhou, Pegah Jandaghi, Hyundong Cho, Bill Yuchen Lin, Jay Pujara, and Xiang Ren. 2021. Probing commonsense explanation in dialogue response generation. In *Findings of the Association for Computational Linguistics: EMNLP 2021*. pages 4132–4146.

## Biographical sketch

Ye Liu is a PhD candidate at Mercedes-Benz AG, in cooperation with Ulm University. She is supervised by Dr. Wolfgang Maier, Prof.Dr.-Ing. Stefan Ultes (University of Bamberg) and Prof.Dr.Dr.-Ing. Wolfgang Minker (Ulm University). She holds double master of science degrees from Tongji University, Shanghai and Technical University of Munich, Germany. She has project experience in automatic speech recognition(ASR) and neural machine translation (NMT) before PhD study. Now her expertise spans over natural language understanding (NLU) and natural language generation (NLG) in spoken dialogue systems (SDSs).

**Yahui Fu**

Kyoto University
Yoshida Honmachi, Sakyo-ku, Kyoto, Japan
fu.yahui.64p@st.kyoto-u.ac.jp

# 1 Research interests

The author's objective centers around developing a spoken dialogue system (SDS) that can emulate the cognitive and conversational qualities of a human friend. Key attributes such as empathy, knowledge/causality reasoning, and personality are integral components of human interaction. The proposed approach involves the creation of an **Empathy-enriched SDS**, capable of comprehending human emotions and circumstances, thus providing companionship and assistance akin to a trusted friend. Additionally, the **Causality-reasoning for SDS** aims to ground the system in commonsense knowledge and equip it with the ability to reason about causalities, such as predicting user desires/reactions and system intentions/reactions, thereby enhancing the system's intelligence and human-like behavior. Finally, the concept of a **Personality-conditioned SDS** involves enabling systems to exhibit distinct personalities, further enhancing the naturalness of human-robot interaction.

## 1.1 Empathy-enriched SDS

Incorporating empathy into the dialogue system is essential for improving human-robot interaction experiences, as empathy is the emotional bonding among humans; robots expressing empathy would give humans a feeling of being understood and satisfied with the conversation. To produce an empathetic response, the generative models encounter the problem of generating safe responses (generic and meaningless, such as 'I see'), or unnatural responses (have grammatical or logical errors, such as 'that is so sweet. I am sorry to hear that'). Instead, the retrieval-based models are guaranteed to produce natural and empathetic responses, as they are retrieved from external documents, but encounter the problem of producing responses that are not closely relevant to the dialogue context. In order to address the aforementioned challenges, the author proposed to combine a VAE-based response generation model with a retrieval system based on emotion recognition. Additionally, the proposed approach incorporates the use of multi-modal facial expressions by the virtual agent to enhance the vividness of empathy. This combined methodology is subsequently applied in human-robot interaction experiments to evaluate its effectiveness.

## 1.2 Causality reasoning for SDS

Integrating commonsense knowledge into the SDS can significantly enhance the system's expertise and enable it to deliver informative responses, thereby serving as a valuable human life assistant. However, in order to achieve a higher level of human likeness, the causality reasoning capabilities of SDS are also essential. In particular, the ability to generate responses that cater to human satisfaction relies on accurate prediction of user desires/reactions from the user's standpoint, as well as the ability to reason about the system's intentions/reactions from a perspective that closely mimics human behavior.

With the advent of large language models (LLMs) such as GPT-3 and ChatGPT, Bang et al. (2023b) introduced ChatGPT's potential in causal reasoning based on whether the model can make a judgment on correct causes or effects. However, existing evaluations primarily focus on assessing the LLMs' capacity to recognize causes or effects from the user's perspective, rather than generating causality explanations from the view of both the user and the system. In this study, the author initially evaluated the ability of LLMs for causality explanation generation and subsequently proposed an approach to enhance this capability through the integration of in-context learning and commonsense reasoning, which considers the system's intention and reaction, along with the user's desire and reaction.

## 1.3 Personality-conditioned SDS

Personality refers to the unique set of enduring traits, patterns of thoughts, feelings, and behaviors that characterize an individual. A personality-conditioned dialogue system that exhibits distinct personalities, can create a more human-like conversational experience, fostering a sense of rapport and understanding with the users. The expression of personality is contingent upon the situation. For example, people may be more inclined to openly express their thoughts, feelings, and experiences among close friends, while in a formal or initial conversation, such expression tends to be politer and more subtly implied. Furthermore, individuals with diverse personality traits tend to exhibit distinct empathetic styles in their responses (Richendoller et al. et al (1994)). Extroverts, for example, may frequently employ positive emotional language and show perspective-taking compared to intro-



*Proceedings of the 19th Annual Meeting of the Young Reseachers' Roundtable on Spoken Dialogue Systems*, pages 62–63
September 11–12, 2023. ©2023 Association for Computational Linguistics

verts. By incorporating personality-based empathetic responses, more gratifying conversations can be achieved. Therefore, the author actively conducts ongoing research in the field of personality-conditioned SDS, which aims to develop spoken dialogue systems that adapt their responses based on individual personality traits.

## 2 Spoken dialogue system (SDS) research

In the forthcoming years, two potential directions for the SDS community could involve the automated evaluation of subjective aspects within SDS and developing personalized SDS to cater to users with diverse personalities.

### 2.1 Trustable evaluations for SDS

In the field of open-domain dialogue systems, evaluation is commonly conducted using automatic metrics and human judgments. However, automatic metrics, such as BLEU, METEOR, and ROUGE, are based on word overlap and struggle to capture the diverse nature of dialogue systems. On the other hand, human judgments are more reliable, but expensive and lack standardized protocols. Hence, there exists a necessity to combine the merits of automated and human evaluations while mitigating their respective drawbacks. Inspired by Giorgi et al. (2023a) who proposed human-centered metrics (such as emotion, and personality) for dialog system evaluation, hierarchical evaluation of spoken dialogue systems (SDS) represents a possible approach to effectively quantify system performance. For instance, at the utterance level within a conversation, to evaluate the "relatedness," "fluency," and "informativeness" of the responses. Furthermore, at the conversation level, it is crucial to evaluate whether the responder demonstrates a distinct personality and exhibits empathy appropriately. Lastly, at the system level, the evaluation should consider the system's ability to maintain robustness across interactions with users possessing diverse personalities. However, since all the above evaluation aspects are subjective, the research of suitable automated metrics requires further exploration.

### 2.2 User-adaptable SDS

Humans with different personalities have varied preferences for systems personalities, therefore, a personalized SDS that is adaptable to the user's personality is essential to improve human-robot interactions. This involves a three-step process: firstly, accurately detecting the user's personality, the accuracy of personality (such as big-five traits) recognition is still not good even with the assistance of LLMs; secondly, exploring the mapping between user personality traits and corresponding system personalities in both chit-chatting and task-oriented domains; and finally, personalized response generation which is tailored to the user's unique personality. Moreover, for the purpose of achieving a higher level of human likeness, it is crucial to incorporate a fusion of verbal and non-verbal response generation techniques within the system. This entails the inclusion of elements such as backchannels, fillers, pitch variations, facial expressions, and other relevant non-verbal cues. By incorporating these steps, the SDSs are expected to effectively cater to the individual preferences of users, thereby improving the overall interaction experience.

## 3 Suggested topics for discussion

- What are the subsequent advancements in commonsense/knowledge reasoning for SDS, and how can they be effectively applied to various SDS tasks?
- The interplay between personality and emotion in personality recognition and response generation.
- In what ways can an empathy-enriched SDS contribute to the treatment and management of mental disorders?

## Acknowledgements

This work was supported by JSPS KAKENHI (JP19H05691), and JST Moonshot R&D (JPMJPS2011). This work was also supported by JST, the establishment of university fellowships towards the creation of science technology innovation, Grant Number JPMJFS2123.

## References

Richendoller Nadine R et al. 1994. Exploring the links between personality and empathic response style. *Personality and individual Differences* 17(3):303–311.

Salvatore Giorgi et al. 2023a. Human-centered metrics for dialog system evaluation. *arXiv preprint arXiv:2305.14757* .

Yejin Bang et al. 2023b. A multitask, multilingual, multimodal evaluation of chatgpt on reasoning, hallucination, and interactivity. *arXiv preprint arXiv:2302.04023* .

## Biographical sketch

Yahui Fu is currently pursuing a Ph.D. degree at the Department of Intelligence Science and Technology, Kyoto University, Kyoto, Japan. She received M.S. degrees from both Tianjin University, Tianjin, China, and the Japan Advanced Institute of Science and Technology, Ishikawa, Japan, in 2021. Additionally, she is currently a research intern at rinna Co., Ltd. in Japan. Her research interests include spoken dialogue systems and multimodal emotion recognition.

# Ryu Hirai

Nagoya University
Nagoya, Aichi
Japan
hirai.ryu.k6
@s.mail.nagoya-u.ac.jp


## 1 Research interests

Although task-oriented dialogue systems have improved, not all users can accomplish their tasks (Takanobu et al., 2020). The task success rate of the state-of-the-art model (Feng et al., 2023) on the MultiWOZ dataset (Budzianowski et al., 2018) is around 80%, indicating room for improvement. Even for dialogue systems built using large language models such as OpenAI's ChatGPT[1], the system performance is not always satisfactory (Hudeček and Dušek, 2023). One possible reason for this limited performance is that users fail to achieve their tasks because of limited knowledge about the system. Hence, I seek to offer a solution based on **tutorials**, which provide users with system knowledge, and **user adaptation**, which adapts the system's behavior to that of the user, thus enabling users to succeed in dialogues without changing their behavior.

### 1.1 Tutorials in task-oriented dialogue systems

To develop appropriate tutorials, I am currently conducting studies on estimating a user's task success ability. Among previous studies on user ability estimation, Ghazarian and Noorhosseini (2010) constructed an automatic skill classifier that uses mouse movements in desktop applications to adjust the interface or content provided by the system. Komatani et al. (2003) proposed a method for estimating user attributes, such as the skill level with respect to a system, and enabling the system to change its behavior accordingly. However, those studies focused on estimating user ability solely from user behavior. I believe that consideration of the characteristics of users' tasks would lead to better user ability estimation.

I proposed a method that estimates task success ability by applying item response theory (IRT) (Lord, 1980), which is commonly used in education for estimating examinee abilities, in slot-filling task-oriented dialogue systems (Hirai et al., 2023). Specifically, I first collect dialogues in which the system presents each user with a unique dialogue goal and the user must engage in a dialogue based on that goal. Next, by treating the correct filling of each designated slot as a problem, I apply IRT to estimate the item characteristics of slots. Finally, the user engages in the dialogue based on the given goal, and his/her task success ability is estimated by using the item characteristics of filled and unfilled slots. Through experiments on using the estimated task success ability to predict the probability of a correct answer for each slot, I found that the proposed method significantly outperformed baseline methods. In other words, the proposed method could accurately estimate a user's task success ability.

I now seek to improve the estimation accuracy by applying recent deep-learning-based IRT methods. Additionally, I aim to investigate methods for estimating task success ability more efficiently by not requiring the user to engage in a complete dialogue. I also want to create an interactive tutorial agent that poses a user with a certain dialogue goal and estimates the user's task success on the basis of how the goal is handled.

### 1.2 User adaptation by task-oriented dialogue systems

Tutorials can enable users to achieve tasks by changing their behavior. In an engineering sense, however, it is desirable to not require users to change their behavior, which makes user adaptation a viable option. That is, if a system can vary its behavior according to the user, then users will be able to accomplish tasks more easily.

I am particularly interested in exploring methods to adapt the system behavior according to a user's task success ability. For example, I want to develop a system that leverages a user's estimated task success ability to change the vocabulary level, adjust the amount of information included in an utterance, or adapt the parameters of recognition models such as those used in speech recognition and natural language understanding. For instance, Ohashi and Higashinaka (2022) proposed a method that uses reinforcement learning to generate adaptive utterances for users with a limited vocabulary. Such techniques using reinforcement learning could be applied in this research.

I previously participated in the Dialogue Robot Competition 2022 (DRC2022) (Minato et al., 2022). In that competition, participants developed systems for humanoid robots in a physical environment to act as counter

[1] https://openai.com/blog/chatgpt/



*Proceedings of the 19th Annual Meeting of the Young Reseachers' Roundtable on Spoken Dialogue Systems*, pages 64–65
September 11–12, 2023. ©2023 Association for Computational Linguistics

salespeople for travel agencies. I consider this setting ideal for developing user-adaptive task-oriented dialogue systems, because many types of users visit travel agencies, and salespeople must exhibit hospitality and adapt to users as much as possible to enable them to accomplish tasks in an efficient, satisfactory manner. In addition to the robot's dialogue content, I also want to implement multi-modal, user-dependent behaviors such as gestures and facial expressions.

## 2 Spoken dialogue system (SDS) research

Multi-modal dialogue systems have the characteristic of being able to convey information that cannot be conveyed through text or speech alone. However, the research on multi-modal dialogue systems is not especially extensive when compared with research on text- or speech-based dialogue systems. Additionally, most of the current research on multi-modal dialogue systems focuses on systems that use images (Sun et al., 2022), whereas there is limited research on dialogue robots in physical environments.

I believe that the scarcity of large-scale, multi-modal dialogue datasets is one reason for the limited progress in the field. It is anticipated that virtual-, augmented-, or mixed-reality systems will be useful in constructing multi-modal dialogue datasets at a lower cost, thus enabling the development of large multi-modal datasets. Consequently, there will be an increase in research on multi-modal dialogue systems, including those involving robots.

## 3 Suggested topics for discussion

I would like to discuss the following topics:

- What information should be obtained from users when adapting task-oriented dialogue systems to them?
- Deep learning is commonly used in task-oriented dialogue systems but involves high costs for dataset construction. What methods are available to collect annotated, large-scale datasets efficiently?
- Can large language models be used for accurate annotation of task-oriented dialogue datasets?

## References


Paweł Budzianowski, Tsung-Hsien Wen, Bo-Hsiang Tseng, Iñigo Casanueva, Stefan Ultes, Osman Ramadan, and Milica Gašić. 2018. MultiWOZ — a large-scale multi-domain Wizard-of-Oz dataset for task-oriented dialogue modelling. In *Proc. of EMNLP*. pages 5016–5026.

Yihao Feng, Shentao Yang, Shujian Zhang, Jianguo Zhang, Caiming Xiong, Mingyuan Zhou, and Huan Wang. 2023. Fantastic Rewards and How to Tame Them: A Case Study on Reward Learning for Task-oriented Dialogue Systems. *arXiv preprint arXiv:2302.10342* .

Arin Ghazarian and S Majid Noorhosseini. 2010. Automatic detection of users' skill levels using high-frequency user interface events. *User Modeling and User-Adapted Interaction* 20:109–146.

Ryu Hirai, Ao Guo, and Ryuichiro Higashinaka. 2023. Applying Item Response Theory to Task-oriented Dialogue Systems for Accurately Determining User's Task Success Ability. In *Proc. of SIGDIAL*.

Vojtěch Hudeček and Ondřej Dušek. 2023. Are LLMs All You Need for Task-Oriented Dialogue? *arXiv preprint arXiv:2304.06556* .

Kazunori Komatani, Shinichi Ueno, Tatsuya Kawahara, and Hiroshi G Okuno. 2003. User Modeling in Spoken Dialogue Systems for Flexible Guidance Generation. In *Proc. of Eurospeech*. pages 745–748.

Frederic M Lord. 1980. *Applications of Item Response Theory to Practical Testing Problems*. Routledge.

Takashi Minato, Ryuichiro Higashinaka, Kurima Sakai, Tomo Funayama, Hiromitsu Nishizaki, and Takayuki Nagai. 2022. Overview of Dialogue Robot Competition 2022. *arXiv preprint arXiv:2210.12863* .

Atsumoto Ohashi and Ryuichiro Higashinaka. 2022. Adaptive Natural Language Generation for Task-oriented Dialogue via Reinforcement Learning. In *Proc. of COLING*. pages 242–252.

Qingfeng Sun, Yujing Wang, Can Xu, Kai Zheng, Yaming Yang, Huang Hu, Fei Xu, Jessica Zhang, Xiubo Geng, and Daxin Jiang. 2022. Multimodal Dialogue Response Generation. In *Proc. of ACL*. pages 2854–2866.

Ryuichi Takanobu, Qi Zhu, Jinchao Li, Baolin Peng, Jianfeng Gao, and Minlie Huang. 2020. Is Your Goal-Oriented Dialog Model Performing Really Well? Empirical Analysis of System-wise Evaluation. In *Proc. of SIGDIAL*. pages 297–310.


## Biographical sketch

Ryu Hirai is a master's student at the Graduate School of Informatics, Nagoya University. He is interested in making task-oriented dialogue systems user-friendly and participated in the Dialogue Robot Competition 2022. He is supervised by Prof. Ryuichiro Higashinaka.

# Author Index

**Association for Computational Linguistics**
209 N. Eighth Street
Stroudsburg, Pennsylvania 18360

ISBN 978-1-7138-9066-9

9 781713 890669

CURRAN ASSOCIATES INC.
proceedings.com

# Workshop on Automatic Summarization for Creative Writing 2022

Gyeongju, South Korea
17 October 2022